LOVE IS STRONGER THAN DEATH

LOVE IS STRONGER THAN DEATH

The Mystical Union of Two Souls

CYNTHIA BOURGEAULT

BELL TOWER ✠ NEW YORK

Some of the material in this book first appeared in slightly different form in *Gnosis* magazine, winter 1997, and in *Common Boundary,* summer 1999.

A complete listing of permissions to reprint previously published material appears on page 223.

Published by Bell Tower, 201 East 50th Street, New York, New York 10022. Member of the Crown Publishing Group.

Random House, Inc. New York, Toronto, London, Sydney, Auckland
www.randomhouse.com

Bell Tower and colophon are registered trademarks of Random House, Inc.

Printed in the United States of America

Design by Barbara Balch

Library of Congress Cataloging-in-Publication Data
Bourgeault, Cynthia.
    Love is stronger than death : the mystical union of two souls /
Cynthia Bourgeault. — 1st ed.
        p.   cm.
    Includes bibliographical references.
      1. Bourgeault, Cynthia.   2. Future life—Christianity.
    3. Love—Religious aspects—Christianity.   I. Title.
BT902.B67   1999
283'.092—dc21
[B]   98-56526
                                                        CIP

ISBN 0-609-60473-2

10 9 8 7 6 5 4 3 2 1

First Edition

FOR LOUIS NUMA ROBIN JR.

Here and there does not matter.
We must be still and still moving
Into another intensity
For a further union, a deeper communion.

T. S. ELIOT, *Four Quartets*

Contents

7

In Gratitude

FIRST AND FOREMOST, to the monks of St. Benedict's Monastery, Snowmass, Colorado, and especially to their remarkable abbot, Father Joseph Boyle, who made space for Rafe and me to walk out the last leg of Rafe's human journey together, and who after his death supported me in my grief to the very best of their understanding and compassion.

To those special friends who held my story close to their hearts and encouraged me to keep following wherever love led: Michael Boudreaux, Barbara and Bill Howell, Jessa Watkins, Father Dan Kelliher, Sarah Barton, Margaret Haines, and my two daughters and sons-in-law, Gwen and Rod Rehnborg and Lucy and Alby King.

To those who helped out financially during the writing of this book: Kathy and Bill Bauer, Ellen and Bill Hunt, Tony Burkart, and many other wonderful people in the Episcopal Diocese of Colorado and the Contemplative Society of British Columbia.

To Richard Smoley, who published my first attempt to tell this story as an article in the winter 1997 issue of *Gnosis* magazine; and to Toinette Lippe of Bell Tower, who recognized it as a book and brought it to its final form. To Charles Upton and Jennifer Doane, who generously shared with me their own work-in-progress on courtly love; and to Brother David Steindl-Rast and Andrew Harvey, whose willingness to go to bat for a risky manuscript by an unknown author made a crucial difference to its seeing the light of day.

To Sarah B. Wheeler of Sounds True in Boulder, Colorado, for so many fruitful connections.

And finally, to members of Rafe's immediate family—Tommy, Helen, and Sister Helene Robin; Brother Laurin Hartzog; and Shirley Powell—who welcomed me into their homes and shared many intimate pieces of their family history that have helped me to understand so much better the man I am privileged to call friend, teacher, and beloved.

Foreword

YOU ARE ABOUT TO READ A LOVE STORY. True, this account is not easy to classify, but with its boy-meets-girl plot—refreshingly told from the girl-meets-boy perspective—a love story it is. Who can pigeonhole love stories anyway? I like to group them according to the four seasons of the year, of a lifetime, of kisses. Each season of love has its distinctive kisses: the awkward, teeth-bumping kisses of sweet breath springtime; summer kisses burning with passion; the kisses of harvest time heavy with memories; and those tenderest kisses of snowflakes on parted lips which delight our second childhood as they delighted our first one.

The love story you are about to read bears buds, blossoms, and fruit, all at once, like the branch of an orange tree fragrant with bloom and heavy with yield at the same time. There is a spring-like briskness to the way Cynthia Bourgeault makes the plot sparkle at every turn like a freshly minted penny. The falling in love of these two mature adults does not lack the giddy dizziness of a first falling, yet they manage to transform the momentum of that headlong plunge into a rising in love. Theirs is a verdant rising: not a rocket-like lift-off, but the gnarled growing of a tree that stretches so high into the summer sky precisely because it is so deeply rooted. Two unlikely lovers—Rafe, a Trappist hermit, and Cynthia, an Episcopal priest—they explore together not just the heights but also the depth of their trust that "God is love: and those who abide in love abide in God, and God in them" (1 John 4:16). To abide in love means to keep on growing, willing to suffer all the growing pains. As we read on, we see how the two begin to reap the harvest by becoming real people. They refuse to count the cost, minding less and less how much it hurts to become real. We watch them laugh and cry their way into realms of which T. S. Eliot says, "We must be still and still moving/Into another intensity/For a further union, a deeper communion...." ("East Coker," V). Inescapably this autumnal journey is bound to lead into the dead of winter.

While it is true that every good love story embraces all four seasons, and this one does, too, *Love Is Stronger Than Death* celebrates, above all, winter. Tracks of snowmobiles crisscross the scenes of this narrative. Its lovers wear heavy boots, and the footprints they leave in mud and snow are inseparable from the trail their story leaves on these pages. Their first meeting happens on a clear, cold winter day; their last one, too. Winter is a time of crisis, sifting out what must die from what will survive. Their love survives and becomes ever more truly itself after one of them dies. "Love is most nearly itself/When here and now cease to matter" (T. S. Eliot, "East Coker," V). With the experience of this truth, the book reaches its high point and pushes current notions about life-beyond-death to an exciting new level. The author makes a unique contribution to this area, a contribution that is likely to stimulate discussion and to startle some readers.

Winter is a time of deprivation, of bereavement. Rilke says of it: "One among winters is so endlessly winter/That, if you winter through that one, your heart will forever endure" (*Sonnets to*

Orpheus: II). And he admonishes lovers: "Be ahead of all winter!" The lovers of this story are "ahead of winter"; they prepare themselves for the winter of their love in the midst of a wintery setting. The snowdrifts of their Rocky Mountain surroundings become an unintentional metaphor for the winter of their monastic environment. Reading between the lines, one is confirmed in the suspicion that monastic life in the West has reached the dead of winter—a creek thickly frozen over but flowing powerfully underneath, ice cracking everywhere. Fierce frost splits even rock. None of our structures is indestructible. But here, too, winter sifts out what is vital from what is bound to die. As Thomas Merton said, only hours before his death, the monastic longing for total transformation "cannot be extinguished. It is imperishable. It represents an instinct of the human heart."

Following that perennial instinct, driven by their passion for becoming real at last, the lovers in this story are genuine monastics, no matter how startling their relationship. They are "ahead of all winter" and are already searching for "next year's language"—one of their favorite concepts. Those of us who remember Trappist ascetics in perpetual silence and strict enclosure may be shocked at a hermit sipping cappuccino in his cell with a woman. I myself am a hermit and I must admit that I skipped a breath. No more than that, though: after all, a hermit does not cut connections, but explores unconventional ways of connecting. My own are internal connections, but what matters is the intensity, not the form. If we need to get shocked in order to drop romantic notions of what is and what isn't monastic, this will be a healthy shock. One thing is certain: This is not an anti-monastic book. On the contrary. It is ablaze with passion for the one essential task of the monk: total inner transformation. This love story deserves a place in every monastic library. It is an exploration of the monk's pursuit at its daring best.

Cynthia Bourgeault faces the difficult task of letting us see "pentecostal fire/In the dark time of year," bringing to mind T. S. Eliot's mid-winter imagery in "Little Gidding." In order to tell a story in which "between melting and freezing/The soul's sap quivers," she adopts an intriguing format. Fluid narrative sections alternate with crystalline speculative reflections. Although these reflective passages draw on Gurdjieff, Jacob Boehme, and other unconventional sources, the theological underpinnings of this book are sound. Its spirituality, far from violating monastic tradition, pushes the understanding of traditional values higher and deeper. Let me quote a passage on celibacy to show what I mean:

> Celibacy must be *purified* of avarice and self-protectiveness: that part which would hold itself back from complete self-giving in order to protect its own spiritual self-interests.... That was the "narrow spot" Rafe and I always found the most challenging to negotiate: how to embrace a celibacy that was not at the same time a withholding of self, a flight into holiness; but was a complete and shared realization of "everything that could be had in a hug..." But it does exist. There is a celibacy which is a complete outpouring of sexual passion at a level so high and intense that every fiber of one's being is flooded with beatitude.

I feel tempted to quote at greater length, but this is unnecessary since an index is provided to assist serious students of spirituality. So I leave you to find for yourself what will help you on your own journey of love beyond death.

Brother David Steindl-Rast, OSB
Mount Saviour Monastery, Pine City, New York

Introduction

WHEN SOMEONE YOU LOVE DIES, you weep, you remember your times together, you hold the pieces close to your heart for a while. But finally you let go and move on with life.

In most cases this is probably the best thing to do. But not always.

In certain, perhaps rare, love relationships, instead of the normal imperative for letting go and getting on with life, there are subtle but clear signs that the journey with one's beloved continues beyond the grave. Rather than ending, the walk together is only just getting under way. This is the stuff of mythology and high romance: the Orpheus journey, *The Divine Comedy*. But it also happens to real people. I know this because I am one of them.

My partner in this enterprise is not a husband or even a lover in the usual sense of the word, but a Trappist hermit monk who was my close friend and spiritual teacher. His religious name was Raphael. He was as surprised as I was to be called into this sort of relationship, but we both sensed it as a call and felt that it was imperative to accept it and learn to live it out. Even while he was still alive, he said it would be a partnership "from here to eternity," and this was not just romantic talk, but something he knew from his sixth sense as a solitary and contemplative.

If there is a reason Raphael and I were called in this way, I hope it is not presumptuous to say that it was to walk this path consciously and intentionally. Far more often than is generally acknowledged, those whose love for one another is marked by a particular intimacy and spiritual kinship are invited to continue together beyond the grave. Such unions—sometimes known as "eternal marriages"—come into existence because they are part of the divine scheme. True love expresses the sacred promise that love is stronger than death. And in going the distance on this promise, the two beloveds drink deeply of that complete self-surrender in love that is at the heart of all spiritual experience. In a particularly pointed way, they follow the pattern of Christ.

That this path remains largely unrecognized and the invitation declined is, I suspect, a combination of three factors. First is a general cultural distrust of erotic love as a true path to God—an unease that has rankled ever since Plato and continues to dominate Christian theological thinking, whose spiritual mainstream has been overwhelmingly male, celibate, and clerical. This deeply embedded prejudice culminates in the all-too-frequent assertion that erotic love is a different kind of love altogether from God's love for us and therefore essentially useless as a spiritual path.

The second is an ambivalent and sloppy theology of death, which allows to stand unchallenged the assertions that the dead have "gone to their rest," that "their work is done," and that they "sleep in peace." While the intent of this is to reassure people, the subliminal message is that the dead are in cold storage, removed from all human involvement.

The third is the current insistence on having "clear boundaries" and a "healthy sense of self" in relationships—priorities that, however laudable, make it difficult to connect with the ancient teachings which claim that the very purpose of true love is to form a whole that is greater than the sum of its parts and, through the strength of that union, impervious to death. The very idea smacks of codependency.

Yet these teachings do exist, and the invitation is real. There is a little known but ample body of knowledge in the Christian inner tradition that supports the possibility the heart already intuits: the death of a beloved does not mean the end of a relationship, but simply a new and more subtle phase of the walk together. If the willingness is there, love can continue to grow—and not only will the couple's love for each other increase, but *they themselves* will grow within it as they continue to participate as equals in the open-ended adventure of their ongoing life together.

The walk is difficult—not without its frustrations and anguish. It requires fidelity, faith, and the willingness to bear the obvious burdens of the lack of human partnership and a heart wide open to heaven. But for those able to pay the price, it is a precious opportunity to discover for oneself that true love really *is* eternal.

In this book I hope to sketch out certain aspects of the path as I have walked it so far with Raphael. My aim here—admittedly tricky to bring off—is to steer a middle course between theory and practice and between personal narrative and spiritual reflection. It is neither appropriate nor necessary to share this story simply as a personal memoir. But the teachings that support the principles of soulwork beyond the grave—and my real point in writing this book is to share these—come largely from the Christian esoteric tradition and can appear abstract and convoluted when not grounded in human flesh and blood. That is the difficult balance I am trying to keep.

My hope is that couples reading this book will be encouraged to recognize the eternal elements in their relationships and prepare in the time of their physical life for the possibility of continuing the relationship beyond the grave if the invitation is extended. For those not so called, my hope is that this book may help them to be more compassionate with those who are; and for those readers who are outright skeptical, to suggest that at that tricky junction where spiritual yearning and human desire suddenly meet in the person of a human beloved, "there are more things in heaven and earth than are dreamt of in your philosophy."

In conclusion, I can only say that I accept full responsibility for telling a story that belongs equally to one no longer in the flesh— particularly inasmuch as he was a monk, and of all monks the most private. My sense that he is a willing participant in this project is, I recognize, part of my own circular logic and will rise or fall on the strength of its own truth. I would like to ask forgiveness of those most closely affected—his monastic brothers and his family—if I have inadvertently tarnished the memory of a man who was a dedicated spiritual seeker; and of others who were close to him, if I seem to imply that the part of his life that I shared in any way displaces their own. Rafe and I certainly never expected to be called into this kind of relationship, and we both sensed all along that it was more a matter of being entrusted to each other than of falling in love. But having accepted the call to love one another and walk together the final leg of Rafe's human journey, we did our best to honor it and discover its truth. He always preferred to call our partnership "the experiment." This book is another chapter in its ongoing unfolding.

Salt Spring Island, British Columbia
Holy Week, 1998

PART I

MEETING

IN THE

BODY OF

HOPE

FROM HERE TO ETERNITY

When love with one another so
interinanimates two souls,
the abler soul, which thence doth flow
defects of loneliness controls.

JOHN DONNE, *The Ecstasy*

WHAT THE THEOLOGIAN SHRINKS FROM, the poet grasps intuitively. I write as one of a small band of those who have been invited to search for a beloved in the realm beyond death. It was not a journey I ever expected to make.

My partner in this undertaking I knew for the five years of our human time together as "Rafe"—Brother Raphael Robin, the hermit monk of Snowmass, Colorado. In the last years of his life we formed a close and inscrutable friendship: in part teacher-student, in part kindred spirits, and completely devoted to each other. Accepting the insurmountable constraints upon the full expression of our love, we still—in the words of Dylan Thomas—"sang in our chains like the sea."

For a good three months before his death on December 11,

1995, Rafe and I both had a strong intuition that it was imminent. Physically, there was nothing obvious to confirm this. Certainly he was aging, a man nearly seventy-one still living a brutally labor-intensive life in his little mountain hermitage above St. Benedict's Monastery. But it was a graceful aging. He was still wiry and angular and fit to do a day's work. And yes, he had somewhat high blood pressure, and a serious bout with an infection that past summer had hospitalized him for a week. But he had recovered, and while his energy was somewhat fragile, there were no obvious signs of trouble up ahead—only, as Rafe put it, "a growing inner urgency" to complete what needed to be done.

But Rafe didn't live out of an ordinary consciousness. His awareness grew out of the mystical prayer that for forty years had been central to his life. From that center, he could sense the completion and yearned for it. And after two years of intense interaction with him, some of that same awareness was rubbing off on me. I fought against the realization with common sense, but knew it anyway in my heart. We both sensed keenly that the purpose of our time left together was, as Rafe put it, to forge a conscious connection that would endure "from here to eternity."

"Do you suppose that's what we were called together for?" Rafe pondered one day as we were driving back from a doctor's appointment in Aspen. Of that much, at least, we were fairly certain: we had to have been called together; there was simply too much synchronicity to explain it away as chance. From halfway across the continent and against incredible odds, our lives seemed to have been drawn together on a slowly converging course. Before I knew him, I'd lived on an island in Maine where I thought I'd be for the rest of my life. Well ensconced in a difficult but stable second marriage, I tended a small Episcopal congregation as their part-time priest, wrote and edited for additional income, and was slowly developing a ministry as a spiritual guide and retreat leader.

Out to Snowmass in December 1990 to attend a training workshop in Centering Prayer, I found myself one morning in rapt conversation with the monastery hermit/plumber who had come by to thaw out the frozen shower drain in the barnroom apartment assigned to me for the week. It was December 10, five years to the day from the last conversation I would ever have with him. We stood there in the monastery barnyard—I remember he had one blue boot on and one orange boot—and for more than an hour we talked, the words flooding forth from some unknown depth in our souls. Of the torrents of words and feeling that passed between us, I can remember only one sentence—when he suddenly took both my hands in his and said, "It's all so simple, so very simple…" But what remains with me vividly to this day is my recollection of a circle of light that shone out from Rafe and enfolded us both, and the deep sense of comfort and familiarity between us, as if we had somehow always known each other and were merely resuming a conversation that had gone on from eternity.

Back home in Maine, the episode quickly faded from my consciousness. But one snowy February morning for no particular reason I can yet come up with, I sat down and wrote a letter to the abbot of St. Benedict's Monastery asking if there was some way I might return to Snowmass for an extended time of solitude and discernment—say, two or three months. I was astonished when two weeks later he phoned and said yes.

My troubled marriage unraveled quickly. Within a matter of weeks my husband announced that he was in love with another woman and promptly started divorce proceedings. I could have stayed and fought for the house, but what would have been the point? Staking my future on nothing more than a deep inner prompting that the time in Snowmass was an appointment I dared not miss, I packed up my gear and headed west.

I didn't connect with Raphael right away. After that first conversation, there didn't seem to be any real urgency to get to know him better. We were already old friends, and there was an easy sense between us that the details of each other's lives would fill in as they needed to. He'd stop by sometimes with eggs or bread from the monastery, or to work on the old pump that kept the house where I was staying precariously in water. Little by little we discovered that we'd read the same books and wrestled with the same questions. Like myself, he was fascinated by G. I. Gurdjieff, that early twentieth-century spiritual genius who had laid out a path of inner transformation frequently referred to as the "Fourth Way." Most of Rafe's library up at the hermitage (in addition to his Bible and the complete works of Shakespeare) consisted of books by Gurdjieff and Gurdjieff's three most prodigious disciples, P. D. Ouspensky, Maurice Nicoll, and J. G. Bennett. In a self-taught fusion of Fourth Way ideas and Christian apophatic mysticism, his deepest wish was "to have enough being to be nothing."

Gradually over the next two years, as I shuttled back and forth between Maine and Colorado, our lives became more intertwined. One dismally dark Maine winter day he phoned me up out of the blue to see if there was an uninhabited offshore island he might come live on—"to join you more deeply in what your life has been," he said. And one golden Colorado morning that next summer, in the back of the monastery chapel right after mass, he again took both my hands in his and searched my eyes with a look so full of solemn portent that I knew he'd be by later on and the love so long smoldering between us would burst into flame.

Wherever Rafe's intuition was leading him, we both realized that our human journey together would be brief. I closed out the remnants of my life in Maine and headed back as quickly as possible to join him full-time in the last remarkable chapter of his human walk. From June 1994, when I finally arrived full-time, until his death eighteen months later, we gave ourselves fully to "the experiment," as Rafe liked to call our relationship.

Particularly in those final three months of his life, when we both knew with gathering inner certainty that the scepter of death hung over us, we worked hard to set in place a new mode of communication that might guide us in the next phase of the journey. I will speak of it in much more detail later, but in essence this had to do with a radical emotional reprogramming so that I would be prepared to receive and reciprocate his presence, not at the level of memory or sentimentality, but as a raw infusion of spiritual love and energy into my own vital body—"the body of hope"᾽ as he would shortly name it.

"'For certain very high cosmic purposes it is essential that man acquire a soul. The normal way of doing it is through the union of the sexes.' What do you suppose he means by that?" Rafe was fond of quoting from J. G. Bennett's little book, *Sex*, which had become his unofficial guidebook to these uncharted new waters. We both knew it wasn't physical union that Bennett had in mind, but something deeper: a union of hearts that would endure beyond the grave and allow us to grow toward that one complete soul we already sensed ourselves to be. But to get up to speed for this soulwork beyond the grave required a twin drill on my part—one that Rafe had already come upon on his own in his twenty years or so of solitude up at the cabin: the adamant rejection of "last year's language" (any kind of comfortable habit, clinging, or stopping at a lesser goal), along with a stubborn trust in something leading inward. "Your heart must be invincible," he told me, his eyes flashing meteor-blue. "You must trust the invincibility of your own heart."

Were we ready for the moment when it came? Who knows? After a weekend of solitude in his little cabin and a glorious last day down at the monastery in which his words to everyone were "I'm so grateful, I'm so grateful," he was preparing to head back up to the hermitage when he was felled by a cardiac arrest. His heart burst; it was sudden, swift, and virtually painless. Time: 11:26 P.M. At home, asleep, I came bolt awake.

THE WAKE

Rafe was buried according to Trappist funeral custom—simple, stark, and haunting. He was delivered home from the undertaker's on a plain pine board to lie in the monastery chapel throughout the night, the paschal candle burning at his head, until the requiem mass the following morning.

At first I had not planned to attend the wake or the funeral. Since Rafe was now in cosmic space, why celebrate a departed body? But something dragged me there anyway, just as the bells began to toll, and I took my place at the end of the procession receiving his body in the church. Just down from a day of solitude at the hermitage, I had my duffel bag still with me containing a heavy sweater and a pair of bootliners. It was a good thing. I would need them.

After the brief service and a few moments of silent meditation, I joined the groundswell of monks and friends filing past Rafe to pay their final respects. As I stood before him, *suddenly I knew I was not leaving.* It was as if a slight motion of will, not quite a physical breath, jumped from Rafe to me, and neither of us was going anywhere. One of the monks seemed to catch it, too; he reappeared shortly with a piece of cake and cup of tea on a dinner tray—"*He* told me to get it for you," the monk said. I ate my cake and downed my tea, the last bit of warmth I would have on that bitterly cold December night that changed my life forever.

I do not know how to explain this, and I do not want to exaggerate. I stayed there the entire night, mostly kneeling by Rafe's side, my hand slipped into his, in the flickering light of the Advent wreath at his feet and the paschal candle at his head. The last monk keeping watch quit at 11 P.M., and from there till vigils at three-thirty the next morning, there was nothing but love, a gratitude conveyed entirely through the skin—body to body, will to will. For that night I knew no sleepiness, no regret; it was the most profoundly luminous experience I have ever had. All was forgiven, understood, poured out; that which in life had been hidden in the changeability of bodies and emotions became steady and consistent. There was a distinct nuptial feeling to it: a sense that our life together was not ending; it was only now truly beginning. And somewhere in those cold, dark hours, a voice that was distinctly Rafe's came to me saying, "I will meet you...in the body of hope."

At about 4 A.M., after the service of vigils was over, I adjourned to the church reception room where another of the monks brought me, and himself, a cup of tea before the hour-long monastic meditation began at four-thirty. Not trusting myself, I kept the conversation pretty much to small talk, and the whole encounter seemed low-key. Only several weeks later did he tell me, "I loved being with you for that time. You'd been awake all night—you'd been with Raphael all night—and your whole being was just oozing love. It was pouring out of you."

CHAPTER 2

THE ROAD

NOT TAKEN

ALMOST IMMEDIATELY, HOWEVER, that nuptial ambience was challenged. Still half-molten with Rafe's presence from our night in the chapel, I was met at the funeral liturgy the next morning with the usual assurances comprising the Christian understanding of death: that Rafe had completed his work, had found what he was striving for, and was now at rest. Free of worldly cares and attachments—the requiem text proclaims—"the souls of the just" find their "repose" in a "place of great refreshment," where in imperturbable bliss they await the final judgment and the resurrection of their bodies. It was supposed to be comforting, but the raw edge of my heart kept asking, "How do they know?"

In those first weeks after his death, I found myself caught in a cross fire between Rafe asking me to hold on—as best as I could make out—and virtually everyone else telling me to let go. The sense of Rafe's presence continued to gather force, but whenever I attempted to verbalize the experience to a few trusted friends, even in an indirect way, or suggest that there might be a path still to be traveled together, I was met with responses ranging from wry sympathy to shocked rejoinders. Rafe's work was done, I was reminded;

he had been called to higher things. My refusal to release him could only be interpreted as clinging. Not only would it hurt me; it might very well hurt Rafe.

This was pretty frightening. I soon realized that the only category my mentors along the spiritual path could use to compute what I was saying was that of "ghost"—those unfortunate souls who because of the unusual and generally tragic circumstances of their lives fail to make a clean break and hang around to cause trouble. I knew Rafe wasn't a ghost, but the thought that I might be exerting an unintentional psychic drag on him that could hinder his progress in the next realm was a concern I needed to take seriously, and I knew that the safest course was to do my best to release him. My friends were encouraging. For a little while, they reassured me, my love for Rafe would remain jagged and particular. But gradually, in time, Rafe would disappear into God, and my own tightly focused love would follow him there—and find its true home.

Those were the marching orders. And for a while I tried hard to walk down that path.

Marking the way along this journey of release are several wise and loving guidebooks, including the contemporary Jesuit John S. Dunne's haunting *The Reasons of the Heart.* Woven through his philosophical reflections is a poignant story, clearly personally lived, of falling in love and letting that person go. The death he feels is real, and his words ring with an authentic compassion that makes this book perhaps the most eloquent statement of a scenario that might be called "Christian mystical bereavement": falling through the lost beloved...into one's true self.

Yet at the same time these words speak through a filter—the filter of celibate, monastic spirituality, of which Dunne is a true son. His starting assumption:

> If I set my heart upon another person, then I cannot live without that person. My heart becomes divided. On the other hand, if I give my life to the journey with God, then my heart becomes whole and I can be whole in a relationship with another...

defines the inevitable outcome of this journey:

> When I give my heart to my life [with God], I become capable of letting go of the other person in hope....What happens is that I enter into a new relationship with the person I have found and lost in which my heart is no longer divided.[1]

It makes perfect and hopeful sense—provided one accepts that the intimate journey with God and the intimate journey with a human beloved cannot occupy the same space, and that love divides the heart. These statements, I now believe, can emerge only out of a celibate, monastic milieu. They result in an essentially tragic view of human love, in which renunciation, rather than complete self-outpouring, is the price one pays for wholeness.

Yet that is the filter through which our Christian spiritual tradition is channeled, and it is so deeply engrained that to stand against it felt like making myself a rock in a flowing streambed. "Let go!" the wisdom of tradition screamed. "Let Rafe go, let it all go; fall through the center of your nothingness into God; discover in place of Rafe...your own true self."

But every time I tried, there at the bottom of my falling was Rafe himself. He did not seem to be asking me to let go, or to let him go; in fact, when I came anywhere near trying to renounce the whole thing as absurd and getting on with my life, I would be almost literally buoyed up by the lightness of his presence within me and a strong sense of ongoing partnership. Far from a tragic view of love, this seemed to be much more a comedy, in the classic sense of lightness and harmony and a joyous ending brought about through mutual understanding. And this, of course, is what Dante also called his walk with a beloved beyond the grave, a "divine comedy."

Slowly but steadily the conviction grew in me that Rafe and I were indeed living one life. And this life is not simply a re-creation of his life, the master's wisdom passed on to the student, but brand-new territory, in which our untapped gifts and our commitment to each other's continued becoming plunge us both deeper and deeper into the Mystery of Christ—a new creation that remains open-ended for both of us.

So what to do next? Was I crazy? Did he really know something when he said this would be from here to eternity, or was I simply clutching at straws? How do you tell the difference between "the invincible certainty of your heart" and neurotic self-delusion? ↙

In frustration, I finally turned to my own resources and set it up as a kind of Pascalian wager with myself:

> If Rafe is calling me to continuing partnership and I say yes—
> then the world is ours.
> If Rafe is not, and I say yes anyway—then I will have wasted
> my life in a concocted fantasy.
> If Rafe is not calling and I say no—then cynicism wins
> another small victory.
> If Rafe is calling me to continuing partnership and I say no—
> then I will have missed the greatest opportunity of my life.

Laid out in this fashion, my course of action became obvious. The only thing I had to lose by following my instincts was the twenty or so remaining years of my life, and what did that matter, really? This seemed a gamble too compelling to pass up. Despite the majority opinion in favor of renunciation and release, the internal odds seemed strongly in favor of continuing.

This is the decision that slowly took shape in me during those dark days of the winter of 1996 in the cabin buried deep in snow, as I sorted through Rafe's stuff and the shattered remnants of my own life. Why not choose the road not taken, walk it as far as possible, and see if there is a path that emerges out of the promise "Love is stronger than death"? Plus, of course, the presence of Rafe periodically rattling through my life like a freight train left me little choice in the matter. My Greek Orthodox friends assured me this was normal for the first forty days as the soul slowly makes its way to higher realms. But when forty days had come and gone and the communication between us became, if anything, more rather than less intense, I went back to the drawing board, starting with the books in Rafe's and my libraries, to see if I could find anything to help me make sense of what I was actually experiencing.

Bit by bit I discovered a tradition in Christianity whose heart has always been in erotic love and that can proclaim with invincible certainty that the beloved never disappears because the two are two halves of one soul. Some say, as mounting evidence emerges, that the relationship between Jesus and Mary Magdalene was itself a type of this eternal true love[2]—a conclusion that seems to me obvious to anyone reading the Easter-morning dialogue between them in the Gospel of John who has himself or herself ever known a human beloved. As the Church consolidated around male, celibate models of purity, this tradition went underground, but surfaced in veiled form in art, in medieval courtly love, and in the teachings of the hermetic and esoteric tradition.[3] When you fit these pieces together with the erotic love mysticism of St. Bernard of Clairvaux and others (theologically acceptable because the beloved is Christ), a map begins to emerge of the terrain: a picture of how erotic love, the ground of all desiring and the fountainhead of all creativity, is the original and most authentic expression of who God really is.

Could Rafe and I have been called to that path? Is that why my best efforts to fall through him into God kept coming to naught—because we were *supposed* to walk this path together? I still am not able to claim it with certainty. But now I am at least able to claim it as an authentic possibility, a premise that will be validated or invalidated in the attempt to live it into action.

CHAPTER 3

THE MYSTICAL

COMPLETION

OF SOULS

THE NOTION OF MYSTICAL LOVE pervades the whole Christian tradition, of course, from the exquisite imagery of the Song of Songs, to the metaphors of the mystical marriage, the Church as the bride of Christ, and our spiritual readiness as the "wedding garment." There are also human models such as Saint Francis and Saint Clare, or for that matter, Jesus and Mary Magdalene: those whom our hearts instinctively recognize as couples despite all efforts to spiritualize or explain away their relationship. We are reminded of the completing and liberating power of souls working together in a holy love that is in essence erotic. The concept is scary, however, and like a hot coal it is usually touched and dropped.

But I am convinced that the building blocks exist within our tradition to support a working theology of the mystical completion of souls. The hot coal does not have to be dropped; not only can it be accommodated within an illumined Christian self-understanding, but it has important insights to offer that extend and round out our Christian vision of death and the afterlife. For erotic love *is* a holy gift of God. And sometimes this love is so intense and powerful, and the sense of union so strong, that it continues right on growing beyond the grave, knitting two souls into the one wholeness they were always intended to become. Mystical completion does occur from time to time in our human experience, and when it does, it bears witness to those two profound insights at the heart of Christian faith: that love is stronger than death, and that it is the fundamental creative force in the universe.

These building blocks come mostly from the Christian esoteric (inner) tradition—the Fourth Way of G. I. Gurdjieff, plus the lineage of Christian hermeticism, continuing down from Jacob Boehme in the seventeenth century through Valentin Tomberg in our own times. Since many of these names will be unfamiliar to readers in the mainstream Christian tradition, I have included some brief biographical notes on them at the end of this book (pages 195–99). Please bear in mind that *esoteric* does not mean "heretical."[1]

Those readers whose interest lies more in the story than in the theory may find it easier to skip this chapter entirely and move directly to Part 2, which can be done without losing the gist of the narrative. But for those whose primary concern is with the mechanics of soulwork beyond the grave, the following pages will provide an overview of the terrain.

The four building blocks are:

1. The union of souls
2. The idea of second body
3. The vow, or promise
4. "The wonders"

THE UNION OF SOULS

In Christian esoteric literature, the two sources that articulate this concept most directly are J. G. Bennett's *Sex* and Boris Mouravieff's intricate and difficult three-volume work, *Gnosis*. Bennett writes—in that passage Rafe was so taken with—that "the fusion of natures [in the union of wills of a man and woman] is a new creation. It is the true soul of man through which he can fulfill his destiny and become free of the conditions of perishing in time and space."[2]

"The normal formation of the soul in man," Bennett adds, "is through the union of the sexes"—a union, he makes clear, that normally but by no means necessarily involves genital sexual expression. What is at stake is this union of natures, and without such a union, although we can obtain "immortality within certain limits" through spiritual practice, "we remain incomplete beings."

Mouravieff's *Gnosis*, particularly in the later volumes, becomes more and more a hymn to this kind of mystical completion, which Mouravieff himself reportedly experienced with his wife. Echoing an insight whose antiquity dates back at least to Plato, Mouravieff claims that the human soul is "bipolar": there exists in the world a perfectly symmetrical "polar being," who is the unique completion of the other. He explains: "A man alone is incomplete. But just where he is weak, his polar being is strong. Together they form an integral being: their union leads to a fusion of their personalities and a faster crystallization of their complete subtle bodies, united into a common second birth."[3]

While these pieces—from what unknown tradition?—offer tantalizing insights, I have always been a bit gun-shy of them in that they seem to entail considerable risk of diverting the spiritual search toward a mythological hunt for the perfect partner rather than fostering the calm receiving that is at the heart of real spiritual insight. But in addition, these concepts rely on the image of a broken soul: a mysterious bifurcation of that which was primordially one. While archetypally compelling, this concept seems to me too speculative, and too vulnerable to romantic delusion, to offer a really secure starting point.

A more solid foundation for constructing a mechanics of the union of souls lies, I believe, in the inner tradition of the developmental soul. The core teaching here is that man does not start out as a preformed soul (whether whole or bipolar), but only gradually *develops* a soul through a consistent inner practice, based essentially in the development of inner attention and the fusion of opposites within oneself.[4]

This is, of course, the watershed assertion dividing the Fourth Way tradition from classic exoteric Christianity, which assumes a unique, imperishable (and presumably unalterable) individuality, given as part and parcel of life itself. If this latter assumption is true, then the notion of a mystical fusion of persons, through love, to form one soul, becomes an operational impossibility, and the idea of a union of souls is reduced to an exquisitely tender metaphor.

Maurice Nicoll, however, in his book *The New Man*, suggests a way out of this apparent deadlock in his remarkable essay "The Idea of Righteousness in the Gospels." Commenting on the Gospel text "Whosoever would save his life shall lose it; and whosoever shall lose his life shall find it," Nicoll explains:

> "Life" here means "soul" in the original....Translating the word "soul" by the word "life"...is correct if we understand by the word "life" not physical vital life—the life of the body—but the level of himself he is at. Understand that the life of a man is not the outer life of his physical body, but all he thinks and desires and loves. This is a man's life and this is his soul....What a man consents to in himself makes his life and this is his soul.[5]

"From all this we can begin to realize," Nicoll concludes, "that the soul is not something beautiful or ready-made but something that forms itself in him according to his life and that it really is *all his life,* the image of all he has thought and felt and done."[6]

Nicoll seems to offer here the basis for understanding the notion of a union of souls entirely within the framework of Gospel teaching. "A man must lay down his soul [for his neighbor]: and this is the supreme definition of *conscious love.*" That is to say, through a life of conscious love—the persistent practice of laying down one's life for the other, of the merging or union of wills in the effort to put the other first—the conditions will gradually come about for the creation of one soul. As long as the life goes on, in a renewed union of wills, one may speak of one soul, "for the soul is the image of the life."

This union of souls cannot be done out of sheer romanticism, that initial rush of erotic attraction that is all most of us ever know of love. It is not a product of attraction, but rather of purification: the commitment with which the partners adopt the spiritual practice of laying down their lives for each other—facing their shadows, relinquishing old patterns and agendas, allowing all self-justification to be seen, brought to the light, and released. In other words, without a mutual and conscious commitment to bring one's human love into sympathetic vibration with the sacrificial and giving love that is the font of all creation, there is no union of wills or souls. The willingness to die, on whatever level, for the other's becoming is the practice that gradually transmutes erotic attraction into a force of holy fusion.

SECOND BODY

But could this union of wills continue beyond the grave, allowing that one soul to keep right on growing? Admittedly, this idea pushes the limits of traditional Christian notions of the afterlife, but it is by no means unheard of or theologically indefensible.

By an overwhelming consensus theological tradition assumes that when the physical body drops away, the developmental mode is over for the soul, and the evaluative mode begins. Depending on where one finds oneself on the spectrum of Christian orthodoxy, this evaluation can take many forms. In the most rigidly literal interpretations, it means judgment day, with an outcome of eternal damnation or eternal reward.

In the mystical and esoteric traditions, however, judgment and sentencing give way to the more flexible paradigm of conforming to a template. The time during which we are blessed with the external covering of a body is an opportunity to develop the skill of holy discrimination and be molded in the ways of divine love. The seventeenth-century mystic Jacob Boehme is thinking along these lines when he writes:

> God works and wills in…the resigned will, by which the soul is made holy and comes to divine rest. When the body breaks up, the soul is pressed through with divine love and is illuminated with God's light, as fire glows through iron by which it loses its darkness…."[7]

If, on the other hand, during its life in the body the will espouses "evil, lies, pride, covetousness, envy, and wrath," then these become the template, and "vanity is revealed and works in it and presses through the soul completely and totally, as fire does iron."

To conform one's will completely to the template of divine love is a spiritual practice that Boehme refers to as "putting on the body of Christ."

For others, such as Nicoll and Mouravieff, this same notion is conveyed in the biblical metaphor of the wedding garment that constitutes the admission ticket to the nuptial feast.[8] However one visualizes the goal, it constitutes the great aim, and hope, of the Christian inner tradition: that in the course of this life, with dedicated practice, we can develop a second body, "the body of Christ," or wedding garment, which after death enables us to claim a home in heaven because it already bears our human likeness. While not made of earthly flesh and blood, this body still has definite substantiality. Boehme sees it as formed from "the holy element," which he calls "mercy" *(Barmherzigkeit)*—radiant, life-giving love.

But can this second body, this wedding garment, continue to evolve after physical death? Could Boehme's "holy element" be a two-way street, so that the soul beyond death could continue not only to give but to receive nurturance from created life, and to grow in heavenly magnitude?

One who certainly thought so was G. I. Gurdjieff. In his great mythological fantasy, *Beelzebub's Tales to His Grandson,* he speaks of a "Holy Planet Purgatory" where those individuals who have attained an advanced level of spiritual understanding are sent "for a further perfecting...which sooner or later must inevitably be accomplished by every highest being-body."[9] Once a critical momentum of inner development has been attained, in Gurdjieff's view, continued growth beyond the physical body is not only a possibility but an imperative—because the full maturation of such enlightened souls is essential to the maintenance of conscious life on the planet. They belong to what is variously called "the conscious circle of humanity," "the justified," or "the communion of saints."

If these fascinating insights of Boehme and Gurdjieff are true, then it may be possible to envision purgatory not so much as a place where a soul atones for past sins, but where it continues to perfect itself, to rise to its full stature in holy consciousness and love. In the

Christian West purgatory has always existed as a rather shadowy doctrine. On the high side, it contains within it the conviction that the prayers of the living can in some way reach and affect the fortunes of those in the world beyond. This is one of the most powerful affirmations of our faith, that death is permeable by love from both sides! But the tradition has never sufficiently developed the implications of this belief, and purgatory has been flattened by the tendency of exoteric Christianity to compute its meaning at the level of sin and judgment. There does not seem to be enough boldness to take the next step: that prayer, offered in deep faith and love, can transform the very nature of the soul for which it is offered and enable it to grow.

But in fact, Gurdjieff's notion of a "high" or holy purgatory seems to be the logical outcome of a Christian incarnational theology that envisions the highest goal for human development not as a melting back into an undifferentiated unity, but as the ability to sustain the fierce particularity of love. Instead of being dissolved in the godhead, this second body, formed within the matrix of one's unique human creaturehood, grows deeper and deeper in its capacity to receive and magnify the divine light. This, I suspect, is the mystical heart of what the inner tradition means by "permanent individuality."

THE VOW

But it was Jacob Boehme, in a single obscure passage in his *The Three Principles of the Divine Essence*, who finally handed me the key to why this mystery of growth beyond the physical body is so persistently linked in our tradition to erotic imagery (the wedding garment, the mystical marriage, the bridegroom) and to the soulwork of beloveds separated by death. Pondering what might "comprehend"—that is, contain—the soul once it has departed from the body, he reaffirms that under usual circumstances the soul will undergo the process described earlier in this chapter: it will find itself either in hell or heaven, depending on which of these templates (Boehme calls them "principles") it has conformed itself to during bodily life. *But,* he then adds:

> If during the time of bodily life the soul has earnestly pledged itself [to another] and has not forsworn that promise, then the pledge itself comprehends it; otherwise that soul stands in its own principle, whether it be the kingdom of hell or of heaven.[10]

The original German here for "earnestly pledged"—*verloben*—has the connotation of betrothal, leaving little doubt that Boehme is thinking specifically of a love vow and not just any promise. If I interpret it correctly, what he is implying is that under certain conditions ("which we ought to be silent in here," he adds cryptically), a solemn vow sworn between true beloveds during the time of their bodily life can become a "principle" in its own right: a matrix in which their love can continue to grow even after one of them has died and which forestalls the inevitable encounter with heaven or hell. The usual "till death do us part" is replaced with "unto eternity."

A more contemporary way to visualize what Boehme has in mind might be to picture it as a kind of covalent bond across the abyss of death, enabling the two atoms to continue to function as one molecule. The bond is formed through the energy of erotic love.

Whatever image works, the gist of it is that the two beloveds, rather than sealing up the "interinanimation" (in the words of John

Donne) of their souls at death, may under certain circumstances be permitted to keep it open. They maintain, as it were, not two separate souls now separated by death, but a continuous joint account whose language of transaction is through the medium of the second body. The final balance will be rendered at the hour of death of the surviving partner. But this choice can only be enacted if at least one partner (and at least germinally in the second) has developed this second body, or wedding garment, which allows their love to be shared in this new form.

These were the lessons that Rafe was beginning to teach me in our work together shortly before his death. In essence, it was a crash course in building second body, which on the Christian inner path is done primarily through the intense practice of "true resignation" (as Boehme calls it)—the laying down of one's personal will in order to be unconditionally present to the will of God.

In the time since Rafe's death, this reshaping of my will that he set in motion continues in my slow and painful learning that it is only through the development of second body within myself that I can receive and return the enormous gifts of love still to be shared between us. Memory and affective emotion are simply too weak; they eventually break down under the oxidation of time into an aching loneliness.

"THE WONDERS"

"It takes a gambler's heart to do the spiritual journey," Rafe once told me, early on in our time together. And it is gambling I think of when I come to the last part of this question, namely, what is the point, particularly for Rafe, of continuing an open-ended partnership across the vale of death?

For me the gains are fairly obvious, though by no means easy in day-to-day practice. It becomes increasingly clear that the shift of inner orientation that could never quite be mustered by ego alone is slowly being accomplished by love: the shift away from the habitual preoccupation with the things of this life. For as Scripture says, "Where your treasure is, there will your heart be also."

For me, thus, the heart is in heaven. I do not mean by this a yearning for death, but more, a kind of detachment that cuts forcefully through the usual distractions and enchantments of bodily life. If I forget the big picture, if momentarily or even habitually I slip into ambition or despair, I must remember—even as a hypothetical, Pascalian sort of wager—that this is not just my life that I am affecting, but *our* life. Despair, cowardice, laziness, self-justification—all those things into which folly might lead me in my own terrestrial corner of life—cannot be the proper response when I remember the one who has laid down his soul for me. In all, it is a pretty good honing to a deeper and more intensive practice.

But what is there in all this for Rafe? Perhaps the best approach comes in an insight by the contemporary theologian Beatrice Bruteau. "Love always seeks the ultimately *real*," she writes in her essay "Persons in Love."[11] And what is ultimately real in one, she goes on to say, is centered in "an outflowing action of loving other persons."

In other words, love calls forth the reality of the beloved, and the act of loving calls forth our own most authentic and dynamic center. The result is a mutual thrust deeper and deeper into becoming, the unfolding of the wonder of each person.

Rafe and I always noticed that our moments of high striving were somehow less authentic than the messy but always surprising emergences of some unknown new person, who stepped forth, not in the subduing of his or my essential nature, but in the creative tension of a love that cut off all escape routes. What we gave each other was joy and confidence, the seeing and being seen that allowed us to face not only the dark parts of ourselves that needed healing, but those light parts that needed birthing. Our holy substantiality beyond the physical body does not branch off from the highest we have achieved here, but from the *wholest*.

"Man was not born for self-dominion, but as an instrument of God's wonder," writes Jacob Boehme.[12] At the heart of Boehme's complex theology lies the simple conviction that the soul, in its very journey of becoming, is the creative instrument of "the wonders." In its struggle to discover and bring forth what it truly is, it becomes a unique expression of the heart of God, a visible trajectory of that divine, outpouring love that can express itself in no other way. Moreover, Boehme implies in a remarkable passage, it is the strength, the courage, the intensity of the soul's "pure becoming" in *this* world that creates "Majesty," that essential attribute of the next.[13]

This is almost certainly the inner meaning of Christ's parable of the talents, which castigates the one who plays it safe and buries his treasure in the ground.[14] The treasure must come out of the ground; conscious form and shaping must arise out of unconscious fear and impulse; and with gambler's heart and artist's skill, one must play out the hand dealt one by essence. For "the wonders which thou hast wrought and found out here," as Boehme puts it, become the candlepower of the soul whose light is Christ.

With this in mind, I would venture a guess as to what might be in it for Rafe to continue an interinanimated partnership beyond the boundaries of physical death. Strengthened and made one in the body of hope, he and I can continue to work in the wonders, with my corner of reality and his interpenetrating to form a continuous whole. Not by imitating Rafe, but by allowing his deepest wish for my becoming to be the epicenter of my own journey, I can remain faithful to the wonders in both of us that were coming to birth through human love, and they will continue to grow and ripen for both of us.

At any rate, this is the path I am walking, and the road map insofar as I am able to understand it. But I am reminded of Rafe's words, in one of those times of the forgiveness after the storm, "I tried to give it a shape, but it has no shape. All I can do is open my heart more and more deeply."

PART 2

HOW WE WORKED TOGETHER

THE COMPASS ROSE

Lovers—were not the other present, always
spoiling the view!—draw near to it and wonder...
Behind the other, as though through oversight,
the thing's revealed...But no one gets beyond
the other, and so world returns once more.

—RAINER MARIA RILKE, *Duino Elegies*

NOT FOR RAFE, THOUGH. With an utter, passionate commitment to "the thing revealed," which for him was the Mystery of Christ, he was determined that the two of us *would* draw near to it together and wonder, and not spoil each other's view. From early on in our time together he became convinced that the purpose of our human love was to form a conscious connection that would survive his physical death, and to that end he bent his efforts. The four lessons he taught me, which he himself lived well, have in the months since his death become the lifelines by which I thread my way on this Orpheus journey.

I fell into the habit of seeing them as a compass rose, a lesson from each of the four quarters: east, north, south, west. This is, of course, not the way he taught them. Lessons with Rafe were always catch-as-catch-can events, an insight snatched here or there while tinkering with an old snowmobile or feeding a woodstove. But if the format was casual, the content was not. The teachings are uncompromisingly difficult spiritual truths, and on at least two occasions were accompanied by an energy transmission that in traditional terms might be called *baraka* or "infused grace." I say this not to mythologize Rafe, but simply to speak the obvious: that after years of living in intimate proximity to spiritual fire, as Rafe surely had, he had become a bush that burns but is not consumed. Herein, I believe, lies the integrity of the path, and the hope of those who truly embrace it.

CHAPTER 5

THE EAST LESSON

"The Law of Last Year's Language"

IF, ON A VISIT TO ST. BENEDICT'S MONASTERY, you were to drive about a half mile beyond the main turnoff, there on your right you'd come upon a washed-out driveway leading to an abandoned ranch house. The yard is overgrown now, and the dangling barnboard siding and several broken windows leave the house fatally open to the elements. Out front is a large pile of trash and building debris, the remains of an abortive attempt by a new tenant to gut the place and start over. Inside is a strewn mess of smashed cabinetry, broken dishes, and a film of flour and Sheetrock dust, well laced with mouse droppings. It's hard to imagine that anyone ever lived here.

Yet only a little while ago, the Stanley place was a functioning household: funky, to be sure, a real sixties period piece, but with all the comforts of home, even "hot and cold running water," as Rafe liked to boast. For four years, off and on, it was my home. This was the house the monks generously made available to me while I was in transition from Maine to Colorado, accepting a modest rent in exchange for my equally modest efforts to stem the tide of entropy. Rafe was assigned as caretaker, and it was through working together on the place that we really came to know each other.

That first winter in Colorado, Rafe and I spent Christmas together at the Stanley place, to the surprise of us both. His long-established pattern was to be in seclusion up at his cabin from the week before Christmas until well into the new year. But that year, old patterns seemed to vanish in the happiness of the new circumstances. On Christmas morning came a knock on my door, and there was Rafe decked out in his cowboy finery, a box of Christmas ornaments under his arm and a small present peeking out from his coat pocket. We decorated a tree, cooked a fancy Christmas breakfast, and, of course, exchanged our gifts. He gave me an Indian bear-claw necklace. I gave him a copy of T. S. Eliot's *Four Quartets*. We sipped our coffee in the sunroom and listened to Gurdjieff music on my old tape deck while the sun grew round and full over the snow-sparkled mountains, and both of us felt completely aglow in the joy of the day and each other. "The most wonderful Christmas I ever had," said Rafe as he took his leave. The memories of that day kept me going for almost a year, and by Thanksgiving I was already anticipating a repeat performance.

And then, two days before Christmas, Rafe announced he was heading back up to the cabin for his usual time of deep solitude.

I was devastated—as much by the abruptness of his manner as by the actual prospect of spending my first Christmas alone—and tore off down to his shopyard to remonstrate with him. He was readying his snowmobile, a goodly bag of provisions already strapped aboard, and he was in no mood to chat. "But if last year was the most wonderful Christmas you've ever…?" I pleaded. He fired up the engine with a mighty yank on the starter cord and took off. In a rage, I walked home the long way, through the creekbed, dodging the icy branches and brambles that picked at what little was left of my Christmas spirit.

When I got back to the Stanley place, there were snowmobile tracks at the foot of the driveway—and gone again—and the criss-cross marks of Rafe's boots tramping a trail up the walkway. Propped up on the kitchen counter was an old monastery postcard. On the back of it were two lines, carefully lettered in Rafe's inimitable hand:

> *For last year's words belong to last year's language*
> *And next year's words await another voice.*

And below it, as a kind of postscript:

> *Not to worry. All is swell.*

The lines are from "Little Gidding," the last of the *Four Quartets*. I don't know whether he'd copied them from the book I had given him the previous year, or more likely from Helen Luke's essay on "Little Gidding" in her wise book, *Old Age*, one of Rafe's favorites up at the cabin. Helen Luke's profound counsels for "growing into age" had in more recent years melded seamlessly into the already pronounced set and drift of Rafe's life. At the heart of his hermit striving was a continuous self-pruning, struggling to detach himself from the petty tyranny of "habits and emotional laziness," as he put it—in order to make room for something of an entirely new order.

"Don't you see how people who love each other trap each other?" he would snort. "You say, 'I love you,' but you won't let me change. How can that be love? I think that's why so many marriages fail, don't you?"

It had all sounded good when we'd talked about it sometime back in August. But that was August, and this was Christmas Eve, by God! Couldn't he just once make an exception? But already I was beginning to catch on to this most unusual aspect of Rafe's character. For Rafe there were no exceptions. What you believed, you enacted. Period. All the rest was talk. And all talk was last year's language. Seeing what he saw, he was doing what he did. And my gift that Christmas was to learn to live with it.

Looking around at our handiwork that winter of 1995, Rafe and I had to admit that the Stanley place had come a long, long way. Two years of chipping away at it together had restored the place not exactly to elegance, but at least to decent habitability. I had the distinct feeling that Rafe was enjoying the process as much as I. I was the carpenter, he was the plumber and electrician, and we both had a pack rat's mentality. He would bring chairs, a rug, a bathtub—scrounged from the monastery Dumpster or bought dirt cheap at the local recycling barn—and occasionally a real gem, such as the powerful Ashley woodstove in the sunroom, or the matched barstools for the kitchen counter. "What this place needs is a..." he'd start, and the next thing you knew, there it would be—ungainly, most likely mismatched, but in its own way a treasure.

We even had a cappuccino maker—our one brand-new joint household purchase. After teasing me for a week or so about "what this place needs is a real cappuccino bar," he walked in one day and plunked $87 down on the counter—"the whole of my social security," he announced with twinkling solemnity. With that, and my credit card, we went downtown and bought a cappuccino machine, two festive stoneware cups, and a bag of espresso roast. From then on, for the rest of our time at the Stanley, the ritual was to sit at our barstools, raise our cups, look each other squarely in the eye, and offer the inevitable toast: "To the deepening celebration."

But my tenure at the Stanley place was coming to an end. The monks had said I could stay "till spring," and "till spring" it was. There came a sun-sparkled day in May when we raised our cups for one last time. Tears welled in my eyes, and Rafe turned his own gaze sharply away for a moment, then clapped his hand down fiercely on mine and said, "Hush, hush. When the building's built, you no longer need the scaffolding."

"But what about all that we did here?" I wailed. "The love? The concern? Where does it live now?"

"It lives in our hearts," he said, "where it is safe forever."

We packed up my stuff and moved me up the road to a rooming house I had found. May turned to June; the snowpack melted on the mountains, and the floods did what a winter's freezing had miraculously not done—wiped out the plumbing at the Stanley. I settled in, Rafe settled in; life continued. In August, I went back to Maine for a three-week trip. A week after I left, he developed a serious infection, lost consciousness driving his old Scout down the hill from his cabin, and wound up in the hospital for a week. When I got back, not much was said. As noiselessly as mountain summer passes into fall during those early days of August, so our life passed imperceptibly into a new season. Rafe was quieter, he had less endurance, but otherwise was the same old self.

One day, up at his cabin, we were musing about places and things that had fed us in our lives—"the watering places," we called them. Rafe was in one of those sky-blue moods, as frequently happened to him after times of deep prayer, and his eyes shone with a light from far beyond themselves. Suddenly, out of nowhere, he said, "The watering places! Yes, we need them. But we stay too long at them and get caught by them. We forget that one watering place leads to another. They are all connected by an underground river."

We were silent for a while, his gaze trailing off toward Mount Sopris, glistening on the western skyline in its first veil of fall snow. Then, as if the underground river of his own reverie had once again come to the surface, he continued, "The moving of the mountain, by faith. The shifting of perspective to a new way of seeing, beyond attachment…"

"Are you there yet, Rafe?" I asked.

"No," he said, "it's all still becoming…"

The last weekend of his life, Rafe headed up to the cabin again, clattering along on the first snowmobile run of the new season. He was brusque and gruff when I saw him off at the shopyard, in his own space and all eager to be about the new language of eternity. I joined him at some point that weekend for tea by the woodstove. It was a sad, taciturn tea, as we sat in the enormous enfolding space mostly lost in our own thoughts. As I left, he spoke his last human words to me: "You'll see. Nothing is taken away."

By whatever hand of providence, I was not around for the last day of Rafe's life. I had business in Denver and missed what others tell me was a Raphael of utterly transfigured joy and presence. Although my heart, I'm convinced, followed along on his passage that night, the first I officially heard of it was the following morning when I showed up for mass at the monastery to find a note posted on the door: "Dear retreatants, Brother Raphael died early this morning…"

It was the Feast of Our Lady of Guadalupe. Somehow I got through it, even sang the Gloria. Then, dissolving in grief, I headed back to my little room up the hill. Passing by the Stanley place, I suddenly saw snowmobile tracks stopping and starting again, and the crisscross pattern of boot tracks walking up to the house.

In an eerie déjà vu, I followed them up the walkway and creaked open the old door to a room now bare and cold. Instinctively my eyes went to the counter, and there, propped up as before, was a card. But this time it was an Advent card, from a box of yellowed note cards Rafe had up at the cabin, the faded design on the front proclaiming, "Behold, I come soon." Inside, copied in Rafe's painstaking hand, was a poem by Hermann Hesse. The ink was almost as faded as the card; clearly it had been copied a long time ago, somewhere in those years of lonely struggle. Rafe had brought it down for me on the last day of his life.

Here is the whole poem, just as Rafe copied it. It is the "law of last year's language" in a nutshell, the quiet credo by which he had for all those years strived to live:

As every flower fades and as all youth
Departs, so life at every stage,
So every virtue, so our grasp of truth,
Blooms in its day and may not last forever.
Since life may summon us at every age
Be ready, heart, for parting, new endeavor,
Be ready bravely and without remorse
To find new light that old ties cannot give.
In all beginnings dwells a magic force
For guarding us and helping us to live.

Serenely let us move to distant places
And let no sentiments of home detain us.
The Cosmic Spirit seeks not to restrain us
But lifts us stage by stage to wider spaces.
If we accept a home of our own making,
Familiar habit makes for indolence.

We must prepare for parting and leave-taking,
Or else remain the slaves of permanence.

Even the hour of our death may send
Us speeding on to fresh and newer spaces,
And life may summon us to newer races.
So be it, heart: bid farewell without end.[1]

The east. Point of sunrise. New beginning. This year's language. All his life, at whatever pain and cost, in whatever circumstances, Rafe trained himself to prefer it, to habitually attune himself to it. And it is crucial, for the language of eternity is not the same as our heavy, encrusted words of sentimentality and habit, our awkward attempts to love by embalming what we love. On my own, later, I found in Rilke's *Duino Elegies:* "The free animal has its decrease perpetually behind it, and God in front."

I have slowly come to see how Hesse's words are true, and how in those brusque leave-takings that I felt as rejection, Rafe was actually giving me the greatest gift. For none of the journey onward is possible if one is still subtly comparing it to the past, still wishing for a return to the good old days at the Stanley place. Next year's language is in next year's words. And one can hear them and stay present to them in human flesh. But this is at the outer limits of our human capacity and can be done only if one is not at war with oneself internally, but aching wholeheartedly—body, mind, and spirit—toward the new arising, giving oneself totally and unreservedly into its hands.

THE NORTH LESSON

"The Absence of God Is the Presence of God"

NORTH IS THE POINT OF CLARITY, of clear light. Some would call it cold. Artists like it because it shows things as they truly are.

Occasionally in those talks with Rafe I said something right, and this was one of those times. We were having cappuccino at the Stanley, looking out across the mile or so of valley toward the chimney of his little cabin up the hill. I was telling him about my recent small victory in the ongoing struggle not to come up for a visit when he was in solitude. Early in our time together he had welcomed these visits and spent a lot of time patiently teaching me the cabin drill. But after that stay in the hospital, a new factor had entered the equation, and my presence at the cabin was increasingly an intrusion. As I struggled to honor the widening space inside him, this time the strength was there. "I figured," I said, "that if I could love you across the space of a mile, I can love you across the space of eternity."

He broke into a huge smile. "Now you're getting somewhere!" he exclaimed. And then, as if in appreciation, he shared with me a story from his own formative years. About 1971, he told me, he'd left

the monastery in Georgia to head west in search of a deeper solitude. A friend of the monastery had offered a rustic camp in a
remote corner of southern Colorado, and there, uprooted from
everything familiar and totally on his own, Rafe began his hermit
life. It was an exhilarating time for him in its newfound freedom,
but the strain of loneliness and disorientation—not to mention the
sheer physical brutality of the site—gradually took its toll. Late one
afternoon he was out in a thickly tangled, rock-strewn field, trying
to move a large boulder to clear a site for his cabin. He strained and
strained with pickax and crowbar, but the boulder wouldn't give.

"And suddenly I burst into tears," he said. "I was so tired; it all
just felt so lonely, so totally useless. I sat there on that rock and said
to myself, 'Listen, God didn't ask you to come here, you came here
yourself.'

"I'd never felt that way before. It was an ache all the way to the
end of the universe. I realized this must be my 'bare self.'"

Over those next long months, Rafe said, he gradually became
accustomed to it. That ache all the way to the end of the universe
was how things would be, how they had to be. "God can only work
in us through our bare self," he averred. "At that place, if a person
is really willing to wait there, God says, 'Aha! Now we can get down
to work. At last there is something to work with.'"

Later, in an astonishing observation, Rafe added, "We only
think it's bare because the light is so intense that it blinds us."

Again and again Rafe taught me to work this way, not flinching
from those moments of utter unremitting emptiness. "You have to
endure the tedium until something gradually emerges in it," he told
me, the lesson of those long, empty winters up at the cabin. *In* it,

not from it, he insisted. It is not the incubator of the new; it is the new itself, in the beginning of its own true dimensionality, stark and pitilessly embracing.

Sometimes, he said, he'd cry out with terror. With the ache and futility of it. With a life wasted, a God far away. "That's the beginning of it. That's when you're getting somewhere. If you can only just stay present in that bare self, you'll begin to discover how the absence of God is the presence of God."

We are human. We want to jerk away from that moment. Fill it with distraction and activity, with our own meaning. In my case, run up the hill to Rafe's cabin, fill it with a person, sitting in his chair in his lonely winter watch—a person, my heart told me, who would too soon be gone. Fill it with a conversation, a cappuccino, the energy flowing between us, the joy of times shared, the glow of human love. But to live in that world, to warm oneself only by its fire, means to be stranded in unbridgeable, wrenching loss when that fire flickers out. To find the eternal communion, one must not be afraid to venture into that dark, black sea of what seems inexpressible absence. More painfully, one must *choose* to venture out, while the fire is still burning on the shore. For only what is truly begun here can continue in eternity.

Dwell in it…endure the tedium until something gradually emerges in it. Often now, I lie in my bed and simply ache. But I try to remember that this ache is what is given to me in this moment to express the presence itself; to paraphrase Rilke, it is the beginning of a love I can just scarcely bear in human form. In the cosmic sphere everything is a two-way street. By that very ache I know I am still connected in love; it is the bridge on which I cross. I remember Rafe saying, "It seems bare only because it's so full of light."

"If I can love you across the space of a mile, I can love you across the space of eternity." And it proves so, slowly but truly. Many years ago in Maine, I learned this same lesson sailing my boat at night. At first it seems like blinding darkness...nothing, nothing out there. But gradually, if one doesn't panic and reach for a flashlight, the darkness lightens and assumes shape. By its strangely companionable light I continue on.

THE SOUTH LESSON

"Everything That Can Be Had in a Hug Is Right Here"

THE THIRD CORNER OF THE TRIANGLE in which our learning unfolded was at Rafe's shop. He had a fifteen-by-thirty-foot workshop attached to the back of the monastery woodshed, its battered garage door opening out into a shopyard well littered with snowmobile carcasses, tractor parts, and miscellaneous two-cycle engines in extremis. This corner of Rafe's universe was really base camp to support the runs up the hill in winter, the mile-and-a-half snowtrail up to the cabin.

A good deal of the interaction between us—the bulk of it, actually—was simply putting in time together at the shop. We worked along, mostly scavenging old snowmobile parts from the hulks in the yard to assemble one or two machines that would make it through the winter. Rafe would toss a few clumps of wood into the old coalstove, and when it got warm enough to work, we'd set to it. After a while, I could begin to anticipate what he'd need next: hand him tools or spark plugs, or fit my hands into places his were too large to reach. Long habituated to working alone, he suffered my presence more than welcomed it. But when I made motions to leave, he'd start a conversation. "Your hands cold?" he'd ask. "Let's warm them on the stove." Moving over to the stove, we'd huddle in its warmth, talking about this or that. In those moments the gems would usually come, those famous Raphael one-liners such as "I want to have enough being to be nothing."

The south: point of warmth, of assistance from above. The winter sun midway in its course, melting the icicles of the night, filling the earth with heat, from a fire far beyond the earth's magnitude. To receive this fire without being destroyed, to be nourished and incandescent with a love scarcely endurable in human flesh, the bush that burns but is not consumed....

I was a kid of the new school. I thought hugs were good, that there wasn't much that couldn't be fixed by someone holding you close.

Rafe was a kid of the old school. Raised in the monastic practices of a generation ago, and to the very end of his days unreconciled with his sexuality, he had spent a lifetime taming his passions, which he regarded as alien forces driving him away from his yearning for complete absorption in God. Sometimes we did hug, and the space between us grew vast and luminous. At other times he was rough and removed, springing back like a wild animal from a trap. "Just pandering to weakness, pandering to weakness," he'd mutter.

That always threw us into a bad cycle. He'd mock my clutching and clinging and declaim, "Get thee a husband!" I'd castigate his "flight into holiness" and taunt, "If you're such a great hermit, why don't you just stay up there awhile?" In two years we'd been around that circle many times.

And that's how it started to go again, that Ash Wednesday morning at the shop. We were by the stove after a good piece of work on a clutch assembly, but internally things had been going downhill. All through that morning I could feel him gradually slipping away into that "high lonesome" in himself, moody and withdrawn, the place where I could never find him. And as my own sense of fearfulness and rejection grew, I watched it trigger that same dumb move I always made in these circumstances. A whiny little voice deep from childhood began to speak: "Rafe, can we have a hug?"

He started to draw back, as he always did at these times. Then, suddenly, something different happened. I caught it the instant it started. Those blue eyes, rather than turning angry and aloof, became intense and focused right on me as he said, "You'll see; everything that can be had in a hug is right here."

"Don't give me that Platonic stuff—" I began, then stopped dead in my tracks. The last thought I can remember thinking is "Dear God, he's right!" The most intense feeling of union, as powerful as any physical hug that had ever arched between us—far more so, in fact—was all right there. For a split second I felt it, knew it: this was the energy of pure intention, beyond form, inside form, at the heart of it. Aimed directly at me.

A split second—and then my mind shut down altogether. I couldn't finish that thought, couldn't even reconstruct the start of it. Several hours later, trying to replay what had happened, my mind could still only creep to the precipice of it before falling off into nothing. Maurice Nicoll would surely have said that the inrush of energy into my higher emotional center had completely overwhelmed the lower centers. My usual mind was carried away in the floods, like the pump house at the Stanley. The last fact I could hold on to was that the inner essence of the outer hug was there, perfect and in its entirety, the naked thing itself. Rafe wasn't withdrawing, wasn't fleeing into holiness. He was simply sharing with me the full brunt of what he knew: that the outer, physical form somehow slowed down or thickened something that could be communicated instantaneously, as raw intention. That first time, the intensity of it overwhelmed my system. It would be a while before a body of hope could take shape in me able to contain and receive energy in that form.

I have continually resisted the temptation to mythologize Rafe. Partly because he insisted on it. He considered himself—and was—very much a man: not an angel despite the name they had given him at the monastery, nor a shaman clad in jeans and work-shirt, but a flesh-and-blood, fragile human being, struggling against his considerable inner passions and addictions. And yet, it still is true that during those long years of work on himself, he had developed certain powers that were beyond the ordinary, that one might indeed call shamanic. I remember him telling me quite clearly one day up at the cabin, "Ten years ago I would have married you. But I didn't know then what I know now."

What Rafe had learned in those years is, I believe, something of the ancient and mostly vanished science of the transformation of sexual energy.

He never spoke much about the precipitating circumstances. Occasionally pieces of the story would come out, like slivers of glass from an old wound. Alone, still agonizing over the debacle of whatever had happened shortly after his arrival in Colorado—"an attraction," he snapped, "it just sort of ended"...face-to-face with his blind, passionate nature, choosing to cut it off cold—"like an alcoholic can't take that first drink"—at whatever frightful cost to his psyche and that of the one he left behind, he stumbled on toward an unknown God who demanded all.

Out of those years of intense wrestling with his passions, there gradually crystallized in him a certain ability to "put" his soul wherever he wanted it—to travel beyond his physical body through the force of conscious will. Essentially, as I see it, he learned how to tap into the enormous generative force of his unexpressed sexual energy, and through it, to concentrate the whole of himself in his heart and catapult it outward in an intense psychic dose. For, as the author of *The Cloud of Unknowing* describes it, "The heart is as truly there where its love is as it is in the physical body to which it gives life." Rafe gradually discovered the secret of how he could be in close touch with those whom he had loved...and from there, with the whole communion of saints.

"When you're a true hermit," he once told me, "you're never alone."

Others have shared stories confirming Rafe's abilities to communicate himself through concentrated psychic energy. One woman, herself a remarkably gifted spiritual visionary, recounted to a mutual friend that she had come to St. Benedict's Monastery to write her book because she "was given to know" inwardly there was a hermit there who would be crucial to its unfolding. In my own case as well, I am convinced that this was the dominant factor in the move from Maine: in some way or another Rafe called me here, to the work we had to do together. From what he sometimes told me of his night prayer, there were "enchanting" travels in many dimensions, soaring through the footfalls of space-time like the solitary red-tailed hawk always somehow circling just above his head, or the Catskill eagle in *Moby-Dick,* that place where Rafe had read the ink off the page.

For better or worse, we never became really good at the practice together. The temptation of the actual physical person was too strong, and the hugs debate went on to the end. And for him, I sometimes think, it was as if we were meeting in the middle, he a wanderer returning from that lonely mountain. For the undeniable psychic skills he had acquired were still not the whole of him; they had been purchased at horrendous cost to that part in him that had to learn to nurture and be nurtured, to love himself in loving another well, at close hand. As Bennett says, while spiritual practice can bring about "immortality within certain limits," without that full experience of mutual becoming in love "we remain incomplete beings." At least, I pray this was the redeeming virtue in Rafe's and my time together, as we continued to touch and not touch, to sink into the magnetism of pure homecoming, and to struggle against it with all the power of our aspiring.

But we did learn, and gain; and more and more toward the end, that old debate would break forth into a new place, where we would stand apart and pure luminous words and feeling could and did pass back and forth between us. My brother caught it once, as we were doing nothing in the shop one day, just standing by a ladder, talking about this and that. "It was like the two of you were perfectly in sync," he said, "and the whole shopyard was bathed in love." And indeed, in those last weeks of his life, it seemed sometimes that we were talking and receiving miles above our heads, as if, like St. Peter walking on the water, Rafe was drawing me, helping me be lifted up to some sphere where the high-water mark of love never recedes and is always present; where things are known, and ever retrievable, by their pure essences falling directly into the illumined heart. It was that foretaste which made possible our powerful communion the night of the funeral wake.

But perhaps the real foretaste happened earlier, during that trip back to Maine. Unbeknownst to me, Rafe was in the hospital during much of that time, the first three days in intensive care. He asked for no visitors and sent no word. I knew nothing about it. All I knew was that from the start, a trip I thought would be difficult seemed magically supported, one thing leading easily to another. One afternoon, on a beach on Eagle Island, two thousand miles away, I stood facing west and, all of a sudden, out of nowhere, felt my life fill up with hope and strength and joy, a mysterious well-being emanating directly, it seemed, from the heart of the cosmos.

Back in Colorado, back in the shop, after my return, we were working on the snowmobiles, Rafe still moving slowly, tired, distracted. The usual, the flight into holiness, and I started predictably to get clingy. "Rafe, did you miss me when I was gone?" "Nah," he grunted, and glanced at me briefly with a look of complete condescension. No, on second glance I could see it was more a look of deep disappointment, as when a gift one has given at great cost is received lightly, casually tossed aside. He shook his head and muttered as he returned to his work, "You still don't understand, do you?"

THE WEST LESSON

"Trust the Invincibility of Your Own Heart"

EARLY ON IN OUR TIME TOGETHER Rafe used to say "I love you" quite easily and often. But toward the end of that last summer, the "I love you"'s began to thin out considerably and finally ceased altogether. With one exception, he never again said them in his physical life. When I asked him if he loved me, he'd say, "No." He insisted that nothing was diminished. The words, he said, "were all just attraction." "So what?" I said. "What harm can it do?"

But Rafe had no desire to be casual about this. Somehow, sometime, during one of those nights of mystical traveling, he had been given to know the difference between the love he aspired to and this "attraction" stuff, and to understand how far anything human fell short of the mark. After that, the most he would say was, "I wouldn't honor you to call the feeling I have for you 'love.'"

Toward the end, this unresolved tension settled into a deep sadness inside me. I knew that time was running out. I saw Rafe slowly fading, slipping away. More and more confined to the monastery, he'd come up to the cabin when he could manage it, where the usual operations he'd done for so many years—the logging and chainsawing—left him breathless and exhausted. I split and bagged wood for him when I could, so at least there would be usable firewood when he got there. With every new snowfall, a deeper foreboding rose inside me. Soon, too soon, he would be gone, and I'd never even really know where we had stood.

Some partings are heralded, the symbolism so haunting it is impossible to ignore. The day I left on that trip back to Maine, I walked up to the cabin early in the morning to say good-bye. It was the end of July, the summer golden and full in those brief mountain weeks between the last frost of spring and the first frost of fall. Rafe was sitting out on his deck, sipping coffee in the quiet cool of early morning. Oddly, I noticed, he was all in white—white jeans, white jacket, white curly hair, and a three-day stubble of white beard; only his black boots and the blue of the flame in his eyes broke the picture. He was in a gentle space, and we fell into a quiet musing about how the little wildflowers around his cabin had already gone by while the ones in the high mountain meadows were only now emerging from the snowfields. "The life force in them is so strong," he marveled. "They know to work faster because the time is short."

"Do you suppose it's also like that at the higher altitudes of spiritual life?" I pondered, and he leaped to that one. "I certainly feel a growing urgency in myself toward the completion," he said with a force that still reverberated in me hours and miles to the east.

As if on course, fall advanced that year with murderous precision, ahead of itself even for this Colorado mountain valley. There was significant snowfall in September, and a major storm on Columbus Day briefly filled the valley with heavy, sodden snow and issued its solemn portent of winter. Rafe had made it up to the cabin that weekend, and to accompany him in some time of hermit's solitude, I'd also taken off to a friend's cabin high in the mountains, well above the snow line. That Sunday afternoon I sat by a frozen mountain lake already in shadow as the sun dropped behind the ridge, and I painfully came to terms with the reality that could no longer be evaded.

Rafe was dying, I realized. Neither of us knew exactly why, but it was clear that life was slowly draining from him. It was also clear that the space between us was widening. And against this backdrop I had to face that the suspension of the "I love you"'s meant exactly what I had most feared. It was Rafe's way of asking for his freedom back, for a release from our relationship. Was I holding him against his will? Was it time for me to go away? Suddenly the answers seemed obvious, and my own clinging pathetically clear. There was only one thing to do, for his sake and for my own: settle once and for all where we stood with each other, and then—as now seemed overwhelmingly evident—bid him farewell, break camp, and return to Maine.

Slowly, one boot in front of the other, I trudged down the mountain.

He was sitting in his old overstuffed chair by a crackling evening fire, disgruntled to be interrupted, but I pushed on anyway. "Rafe," I said, "I need to know where we stand. If you still love me—if you still want me here—I need you to tell me. Otherwise I think it's time to quit."

"What does your heart tell you?"

"My heart tells me you love me. But your words tell me you don't."

He looked straight at me, and all of a sudden everything that was spent in him seemed to grow powerfully concentrated. When he spoke, his voice, which usually these days was somewhat wheezy, was sharp and ringingly clear:

"Your heart must be invincible. You must trust the invincibility of your own heart."

The sly fox! No, of course he was not going to tell me, take away from me precisely the work I had to learn to do. What did my heart tell me? I closed my eyes and saw the cappuccino celebrations, those toasts as we lifted our mugs and gazed deep into each other's eyes—"Here's looking at *you,* kid!" I saw the groceries delivered, the hot and cold running water, the clothes I was wearing, head-to-toe gifts from him...the time, the kindness, always and everywhere the quality of his attention—even now, both of us, every muscle poised and straining to see what the other would do next.

At this point Rafe was fully engaged, too. He jumped up out of the chair and stood by the fireplace, his hands outstretched and trembling. "Look at me, *look at me!*" he said. "You must see how changeable I am; you must see that. One moment it wants this, the next it wants that. One minute I grab you, one minute I push you away; one minute I hurt you, the next I steal your heart. You must see there is no root in me. How can I say 'I love you' when there is no 'I' who can love? You must see that; you *must.*"

I did. Finally. Lifted my head far enough above my own event horizon to look at him standing there, backlit by the fire, the little sentry at his hermit's post, and to realize that he had spoken his own deepest truth. In his words were contained a lifetime of striving, more than four decades of intense spiritual work on himself, pushing on beyond the usual watering places toward that new man in Christ that ached to gather itself out of his human fragility and changeability. Once, in a moment of intense tenderness, he had told me, "I want to integrate my past, all of who I am, and give it to you." And still, in my own blind neediness, I could only hear the cessation of "I love you"'s as rejection. Now, I finally saw, it spoke to the sheer heroism of his striving.

"Besides," he said as the mood between us softened, "you know that neither one of us is going to quit."

Not words. That would have been a cheap fix. Rafe knew that if I was to survive in the next phase up ahead, I would have to learn to recognize, trust, and navigate by faculties much more subtle than attraction and reassuring words. I needed to move toward a new kind of perceptivity and learn to recognize things directly by their inmost spiritual essence, not their outward forms. But this new kind of perception—"a direct contact with the electromagnetic field of love," as the modern Sufi master Kabir Helminski puts it— is possible only for the heart, not the intellect. Unless I could learn to trust this, I would be cut off from the outset.

The journey is toward the west: into the setting sun, the end of all conventional ways of seeing. In the months ahead, I would be called upon to stake my sanity on things people would say are mad: that a body, lying in wake, could draw me close through a pure gesture of spirit; that I could—then and subsequently—tell with certitude that a departed soul had drawn near simply by the unmistakable quality of his attention; that with his will and heart he continues to shape my life, as I continue to shape his. A vast, invisible universe was opening up for both of us, there to be explored, shared, savored in "next year's language." All this learning lay ahead. But to set out on this voyage, the only possible hope was to know, and trust, that part in me that knew what it knew and could act out of it. Beginning now.

I got up and moved to the window, and Rafe moved to me, and together we looked out at the barest sliver of a moon, cresting over the scudding clouds. "Look," said Rafe, "can you see the full-of-the-moon outlined behind the crescent? That's us."

"What do you mean?" I asked.

"Shhh.... You'll see."

We laughed together and could both feel the joy returning as we feasted on each other's rising hope. Then I stepped out into the night, and he moved silently back to his chair to resume his lone watch. Just as I was pulling the door shut, I could hear him say, almost in a whisper, "You'll see..."

WRESTLING WITH

AN ANGEL

IN GENERAL, THE LAWS GOVERNING spiritual practice are clear and exactly as Rafe taught them: detachment, consent, inner seeing, surrender. He was a tough teacher but a good one, and through that very toughness he taught me things that can be learned in no other way.

But there are times, even in spiritual practice, when you simply have to break the rules.

This is the story of one of those times. I share it with a certain hesitancy, for reasons that will become obvious. Beyond any doubt it was my most painful and disgraceful moment with Rafe, a moment of totally losing it. But in a strange way it was also our most intimate moment and a real turning point in our work together. Through it we both began to understand what it really means to lay down one's life for the other, and to glimpse the tremendous healing power unleashed in such alchemical love—a power, I have come to believe, that holds the key to the continued work of souls beyond the grave. Perhaps not surprisingly, this is also the story of that one exception I mentioned earlier—the last time in our human walk together that Rafe said "I love you."

Rafe was, as I said, a kid of the old school. He had been formed in the classic monastic tradition of spiritual warfare, the subduing of the "passions," as Evagrius called them in the fourth century, which are always disordered and always in mutiny against our true spiritual destiny. Rafe took these lessons deeply to heart. In those long years of struggle against his own mutinous nature, he had learned, like Keats, to stand alone on the shore of the wide world and simply let the ache carry him all the way down, into God—"till love and fame to nothingness do sink."

And I was a kid of the new school. Twenty years younger than Rafe and formed in the psychological climate of our times, I was wary of spiritual practice that buries emotional pain and passion— "the flight into holiness," as I tagged it. My own instincts were more along the lines of those of Father Thomas Keating, my Centering Prayer teacher at Snowmass—"the way to be rid of emotional pain is to feel it." Like most of my generation, when fear or sadness arose in me, I thought it natural to expect Rafe to be "supportive"—to stay near, hear me out, and reassure me with his sympathy and maybe a hug. "Don't you see that by indulging it," he scoffed, "you only make it worse?" Whenever I started to get into a bad state, he would leave. Only later, when something had shifted in me, would he return, picking up where we had left off as if nothing had happened.

We never resolved this tension. Gradually, by working with him, I came around more and more to his way of looking at things.

But so often I felt a deep sadness in him. His unswerving devotion to next year's language, and that constant vigilance against being lured into "a home of one's own making," sometimes struck me as the desert-spirituality equivalent of "making lemonade out of the lemons life has dealt you." "I'm gone as of five minutes ago" was one of Rafe's favorite leave-taking phrases, and there was a profound psychological truth to it. For of course, running with all speed toward the new is also the best possible strategy for outdistancing the flames of destruction licking at your heels. It is as if something in Rafe knew that everything he loved would be taken from him.

When his horse Saddalu had died in a snowfield a few winters earlier, one of the monks went up to the cabin to break the news to him. Knowing how Rafe loved that beautiful white Arabian, his brothers figured he would take the news hard. Instead, in towering aloofness, Rafe sent the monk packing. "What's to be upset about? Horses die; I die, you die; we're all going to die." Three years or more later, recounting the episode to me, his voice still quivered with anger.

I was angry, too. "You just talk that way to protect yourself from hurt," I snapped. He winced almost as if I'd struck him. "You can think that if you like." The look in his eyes stopped me dead in my tracks. If "haunting" and "haunted" can exist in the same look, that was perhaps it—a naked, bottomless grief. But one could never get close to Rafe's grief. I could feel it sometimes, and my heart ached for him. But the anger around it was too explosive. After that Saddalu story, it was a week before he would come near me.

And so when I got back from that trip to Maine, I could tell that Rafe was getting beyond his emotional limits as he shared the story of what had befallen him during my absence. He plunged on with the details of that nightmare ride down the hill, passing out at the wheel of the Scout, hitting a tree, finally fetching up in a barbed-wire fence and staggering down to the monastery. Perhaps we were both in shock. The joy of seeing each other again masked it for a while, but soon we were both backpedaling fast. He beat a hasty retreat, and I lay awake all night replaying the details in growing horror and disbelief.

The next day, we were into our worst ever "get thee a husband" cycle—Rafe in full flight, and me in dazed pursuit. The more I tried to come near him, the more he pushed me away. At last he ordered me up to the cabin, to stay there until things calmed down. He spent the night at the monastery.

I was still sitting there the next morning in his old chair—somewhat calmer, I thought—when I heard the rumble of the Scout in the driveway and, a moment later, the sound of his feet on the landing. I guess he was a little surprised to find me still there, and his mood had by no means softened. He set down the bundle of firewood he was carrying and with a look of icy contempt headed straight back out. I said, "Rafe, please, can we talk?" "There's nothing to say," he grunted, and yanked open the door.

That was the moment it happened. Suddenly something inside me snapped. *"No!"* I screamed, with a force that swept away all inner restraint. I leaped out of the chair, wrenched the door from his hands, and slammed it shut in front of him, pleading, "Rafe, Rafe, please don't go, don't go...." I couldn't believe it, but there it was.

He couldn't believe it either. He stared at me for an instant in sheer animal terror, then shoved me out of the way and stomped down the landing. I lunged after him and locked onto his legs.

That was the start of it. For the next half hour or so, we wrestled. I am not talking metaphor here. We spilled down the landing and rolled and writhed around the yard, locked in a desperate contest of wills. I clenched his leg, his arm, holding on for dear life. He brought his boot heel down on my jaw and twisted my wrist so hard I thought it would snap. I screamed but didn't let go. "You're crazy!" he hollered. "It doesn't matter," I hollered back.

After a while, our combat began to take on a strange, almost surrealistic configuration. We'd wrestle for a while then rest, sitting at opposite ends of the woodpile, eyeing each other warily. Sometimes we'd exchange a few words. "Can this be love?" I remember wailing at one point, and he shook his head sadly. "I'm gone already," he said. "You try to grab me and you're only holding on to yourself."

Then he'd make a move to leave, and the wrestling match would flare up again. But with each new round, it seemed as though the anger had gone more and more out of it and something deeper, almost holy, was fighting *through* us. The image of childbirth went fleetingly through my mind.

At some point it ended. The fight had zigged and zagged its way to an irrigation ditch a little beyond the driveway, and there, under a serviceberry bush, I finally let go. I couldn't hold on anymore; the storm in me was spent, and I just lay there and sobbed. Rafe went a little bit away, stood under an aspen tree, spat...then slowly walked back to me.

Silently, not touching, we walked back to the Scout. "Is it okay to go now?" he asked. I nodded. Somehow it was.

"Rafe, will you give me your blessing?" The words suddenly tumbled out of my mouth...why?

"You already have it," he grunted. Then he drove off down the hill, and I went back inside the cabin.

What had possessed me? I didn't know. Surely it was all over; Rafe would never return....And yet, why...why, as I sat there with my emotions reeling and my jaw throbbing, why did I feel this strange feeling of hope? Why, strangely, something like...pride? Out of the shame and confusion welled up this gathering sense—how shall I say it?—that for perhaps the first time in my life I had done something right.... I sat there with this odd feeling for a long time, until it gradually subsided and I drifted into stillness.

And then, gathered in the mirror of that stillness, there suddenly emerged a face—a face long buried deep in my unconscious. Later, looking back through old journals, I was astonished to discover that I had last seen that face on August 27, 1980—fifteen years earlier to the very day.

The face was my mother's. She was lying in her bed in a Christian Science nursing home in California, dying of cancer. They called it "a touch of arthritis." An inpenetrable wall of denial separated us. I saw her eyes, racked with pain, momentarily reaching out to say good-bye...then drawing back and motioning me away. I stood for a moment in her doorway, then turned and walked out, knowing I would never see her again.

The picture shut down again, almost as quickly as it had formed, but I began to understand. "Do not go gentle into that good night," says the poet Dylan Thomas. "...Rage, rage against the dying of the light." And I *had* raged—for my mother, for myself, for Rafe, for a lifetime of things slipping away through the door, irretrievable and unacknowledged. "Oh, Rafe, *Rafe!*" I wailed aloud. Love had torn out of me that morning the grief I had not known was there.

After a long time of tears—how long I don't know—I heard a rumble in the yard and the squeal of brakes. The Scout was back. Slowly the door pushed open, and there stood Rafe.

He had been crying, too. His eyes were red and tear-streaked, and there were dust smears on his face where he had roughly wiped his cheeks dry. He stood there for a moment, then started awkwardly, "I wanted to make sure I didn't hurt you." We looked straight into each other's eyes, and in the same breath spoke the same word, "Forgive."

And then we both burst into tears again. He crawled into the chair with me, and holding each other, we sobbed out a lifetime of losses and sorrow. And as the words flowed between us, of memories long buried and remorse never confessed, Rafe and I yielded our grief to one another, like frost emerging from the spring earth.

Afterward, when the tears had run their course, we headed down the hill together in the Scout. He dropped me off at my gate, and we stood there for a moment searching each other's eyes. I said, "Rafe, you're the first person I've ever loved enough to fight for."

"I know," he said almost in a whisper. "And you're the first person I've ever loved enough not to run."

Who was right and who was wrong? Certainly we broke all the rules, and I cannot imagine that our wrestling match two weeks after Rafe was released from the hospital did much to lengthen his days. It is a guilt I will bear to my own grave. Or perhaps time stopped at the door of our hearts; I do not know; maybe I never will.

But I do know that from that time on, it was as if all resistance between us vanished, and we carried each other's vulnerability with reverence, like a secret shared in the silence of our hearts. Rafe did not run again. In times when despair and clinging overtook me, he would simply wait by my side, gathered and present, until my turmoil subsided. And as I dared to trust that he was not leaving, I began little by little to release that "winged life" I had been binding to myself so desperately, discovering to my joy that it remained right there by my side. At one point early on in our relationship, Rafe had said, "I want to know what it means to truly love someone." Toward the end, I think we were both beginning to find out. While the struggles continued, we walked those last three months of our human life together in some sense already one will, simply and daily laying down our lives for one another.

"Wholeness," says Helen Luke, "is born of the acceptance of the conflict of human and divine in the individual psyche."[1] But I wonder if this acceptance is truly possible without knowing oneself deeply loved by another human being. If the principal office of love in this life is to "unbolt the dark," as Dylan Thomas has it, and release its prisoners of shame, is this not even more pointedly the divine alchemy of the next, by which our wedding garments in eternity are spun? For as I look back on the time with Rafe, I am struck by the fact that in that pure becoming we both so yearned for, it was not the best stuff in us but the worst that God transformed to make the new person. The very force that Rafe most feared in himself, his "attraction," emerged in the refiner's fire of love as true commitment. And the worst in me, my desperate clinging, gradually melded into something I would never have believed myself capable of—true devotion. It is our dross, reclaimed and purified by love (if we trust each other enough to take it that far), that becomes the living core of our "holy particularity," by which we will always find each other in eternity.

WALKING

THE WALK

CHAPTER 10

THE BODY OF HOPE

"I'LL MEET YOU IN THE BODY OF HOPE." Those strange words that came to me that night of the funeral wake! It was not a term Rafe and I had ever used, and for the first few weeks after his death I puzzled over what it might mean. Then one afternoon I suddenly found out.

In February, not quite two months after Rafe's death, I was walking up the road past the Stanley place when I was stopped in my tracks by what sounded like a sledgehammer pounding inside and a pile of debris accumulating out front in the snow.

"The monks are giving me this place for the summer," said the caretaker of the monastery's new retreat center, grinning, his face sweaty and smeared in dust. "I thought I'd open it up, get a little light in here."

Open it up—the place was gutted! It's hard to believe that a single human being in one afternoon's work could unleash such a whirlwind. Sheetrock and splintered cabinetry lay in a pile in what had once been the living room, along with smashed dishes and trampled foodstuffs that had gone flying in the melee. Electrical wiring hung loose from the ceiling beams, and a spigot dangling on a piece of copper tubing dripped the last hurrahs for the days of "hot and cold running water." The Stanley place was, as they say, history.

"I'll be back in the morning with a dump truck," he told me, then packed his tool bag and left. He never returned. Whether the monks called him off the project or he got overwhelmed by his own chaos, I don't know. It was like a groundstrike, aimed precisely at that spot on earth where its demolition had to be accomplished.

After he had gone, I stumbled around for a while in the carcass of the Stanley. Like debris washed down in the spring torrents, little scraps of memory floated through the wreckage, strangely dislodged and incongruous—a barstool sticking out from the trash pile, Rafe's old pair of work gloves in the remains of a drawer. Still taped to a piece of splintered barnboard, once the living room wall, was the postcard from two Christmases ago bearing the reminder "Not to worry. All is swell." I went out on the deck and dissolved in tears.

That's when it happened. As I wept out there in the snow, I began to notice a shift. Although I was still crying, the emotional sting started to lose force, and a new and tingling presence began to work its way up in me, literally starting from the tips of my toes. I felt like an empty glass slowly being filled with champagne.

In spite of myself, I was fascinated. A sparkling, bubbling life seemed to be pouring into me, filling me with such buoyancy that I could no longer sink into despair. And a moment came when the Stanley place simply fell away, like scales from my eyes, and I was able to look straight through all the relics and memories of love and simply see the love itself.

I got up and started dancing on the deck as in that final scene in *Zorba the Greek,* humming a little tune to the words that went, "When the building's built, you no longer need the scaffolding..."

I knew in that moment that I was sustained by an invisible and intensely joyous partner.

It was my first postdeath encounter with Rafe, but immediately it all made sense. Wasn't this exactly what he'd been trying to teach me? And so here it was: the pure essence of his presence and the immense energy of his love—just as it had always been—only now minus the physical body. So what really was missing? I understood that the groundwork had been laid between us for me to know and receive him in this form. The remaining task has been to get used to this new state of affairs.

The body of hope is so crucial to any understanding of continued soulwork beyond the grave that I need to explain it a little more. I am talking about a subtle body, of course—a nonmaterial, energetic manifestation—and I realize that in even raising the issue, I may be walking into an esoteric quicksand. Already readers so inclined can choose among a profusion of ancient and modern metaphysical systems (I can name five right off the top of my head), and I have no interest in adding yet another cosmology of bodies. But the concept itself is a necessity, for there is not much point in proceeding in such a relationship without at least some rudimentary recognition of what it is that might "embody" us beyond physical form. And so, from as simple and practical a point of view as possible, I wish to describe this "body" as I have experienced it with Rafe.

In a nutshell, then:

- I see the body of hope as a living, palpable, and conscious energy that holds the visible and invisible worlds together. It is the sap, metaphorically speaking, through which flows the higher communion—the sharing of personal love and the building up and unfolding of the wonders between two people. It is what makes possible the intercommunion of substances between two beloveds and the continuing growth of their one abler soul even when separated by death. It is the "holy element," as Boehme would call it, that straddles heaven and earth and makes possible the most intimate connection between these two planes.

- It is not itself the higher person, the individual resurrection body or essential core, but it carries and sustains this core in its full individual particularity and enables it to grow and, when necessary, to configure itself visibly.

- The body of hope is itself universal, but our individual connection to it is made by animating something within ourselves (or "crystallizing" something within ourselves, in Gurdjieffian terminology) that can directly receive it. Traditionally this something has been called "second body," or "the wedding garment."

THE "INTELLIGIBLE" UNIVERSE

A simple way of picturing what I am describing might be to imagine our visible, created world nestled in an enfolding spiritual energy field—a spiritual womb if the metaphor is comfortable. It is indeed an atmospheric layer that surrounds our universe, although it consists not of atoms and molecules, but of consciousness, energy, and potentiality. It is the Alpha and Omega of all created things, out of which our life emerges into form, and into which our form returns when our journey through time is over. The Greek patristic fathers called it the "intelligible" universe—pure, ener-gized idea—in which our "sensible" universe of form and particu-larity is contained. We do not leave the intelligible when we come into form—because it is impossible to leave it; nothing once cre-ated can ever disappear from it—and when we die, the whole of our life is still perfectly contained in it.

Is this why Rafe called it the body of *hope?* Perhaps. But more and more I have come to believe that his main purpose is to call attention to a particular capacity of this body, which I have tried to convey in the images of "sap" and "womb." The body of hope is first and foremost a life-giving body; it flows into and through the sen-sible world with the energy of pure becoming, shaping the course of things in this world as well as in eternity. I found the key to Rafe's insight in a remarkable passage in *Meditations on the Tarot.* According to the author, Valentin Tomberg:

> Hope is not something subjective due to an optimistic or san-guine temperament or a desire for compensation in the sense of modern Freudian and Adlerian psychology. It is a light-force which radiates objectively and which directs creative evolution towards the world's future. It is the celestial and spiritual counterpart of the natural and terrestrial instinct of biological reproduction....In other words, hope is that which moves and directs *spiritual evolution* in the world.[1]

Why? Earlier on in his meditation on force, Tomberg distin-guishes between two kinds of energy, or life forces, operative on the earth. *Bios,* he says, is the natural life force. *Zoe* is the source, the higher or vivifying life.

> It is *bios* which flows from generation to generation; and it is *Zoe* which fills the individual in prayer and meditation, in acts

of sacrifice and participation in the sacred sacraments. *Zoe* is
vivification from above in a *vertical sense; bios* is vitality which,
although it once issued from the same source above, passes on
in the *horizontal* from generation to generation.[2]

The importance of these distinctions is critical. Real spiritual
hope is not a happy feeling based in the expectation of some future
satisfaction of desires. It is rather a wellspring, the infusion of
Zoe—higher, vivifying life—directly into the individual at the
deepest ground of his or her being. It is the living water of John 4,
breaking out in the depths of the soul to empower and restore. This
is the dimension I believe Rafe was calling attention to.

And so the body of hope is really a connective tissue, linking
the sensible and intelligible realms in the dance of love as "pure
becoming." It exists for the sake of this dance. It allows the energy
of divine love to drive deep into the human condition—the theological condition usually referred to as "grace." And at the same
time, it allows the yearning, outstretched hands of creation to
pierce the heart of God and call forth what can only be expressed
in the dimension of the sensible. It is the root oneness and inter-
connectedness of all things in what Kabir Helminski calls "the electromagnetic field of love."[3] And because this field does empirically
exist, all those who have deeply loved—"to the root"—will be able
to make their way to one another in and through it.

MANIFESTATIONS OF THE BODY OF HOPE

Energy

The clearest and most dramatic experience of the body of hope
comes, as it did for me that afternoon out on the deck, in the raw

infusion of vitality into my system. At one moment I am empty, drained, depressed. In the next a new life is dancing within me.

Perhaps the classic description of an encounter in the body of hope is in Dostoyevsky's *The Brothers Karamazov*, in the chapter entitled "Cana at Galilee." Following the death of his teacher, Father Zossima, the young monk Alyosha falls into a semitrance while listening to the gospel story of the wedding at Cana read aloud over his beloved elder's coffin and has a vision of Zossima dancing at the wedding feast, sharing in Christ's first miracle. Alyosha wakes up, walks out into the starry night, and is filled with rapture—"as though the threads from all those innumerable worlds of God met all at once in his soul."[4] Father Bruno Barnhart writes in his commentary on this episode, "In what seems to be an initiation into the fullness of the Holy Spirit by the old monk, Alyosha comes suddenly into his manhood, filled with conviction and strength."[5] "He had fallen upon the earth a weak boy," Dostoyevsky continues, "but he rose from it a resolute fighter for the rest of his life.... And never, never, for the rest of his life could Alyosha forget that moment. 'Someone visited my soul at that hour!' he used to say afterwards."[6]

This episode is a quintessential "body of hope" experience. There is that immediate infusion of energy, and with it a strange sense of initiation—of being connected to one's real identity and destination. And there is that profound, encircling experience of love that brings its own certainty that this is not merely an infusion of higher energy, but the presence of a distinct someone who "visited my soul at that hour." No wonder the story unfolds within the setting of the wedding at Cana, that profound gospel parable of the mystical marriage, for it precisely describes the path that the beloveds will follow as they learn to make their way in this strange new country of the heart.

Tincture

But how do I know this is not "just" higher energy? What makes me so sure that this someone or something that enters is not simply the loving, transpersonal descent of the Holy Spirit, but comes with the particular stamp of the person of Rafe? The answer—and it is crucial—is that the infusing presence contains two unmistakable elements of Rafe, which I will call *tincture* and *conscious will.*

Tincture is a difficult term to explain. I adopt it from Boehme because I cannot find anything else that comes closer to the mark. It means, essentially, the quality of aliveness. Everything alive has a tincture...a musk, fragrance, sparkle, uniquely its own and unmistakable.

That night of the funeral wake, I found myself asking at one point, "What makes me so sure this is Rafe here?" The answer came clear and strong when I realized the feeling I was experiencing was exactly the same feeling as had always been there between us when Rafe was alive. The two of us could have been sitting on the deck at the Stanley with our cappuccino mugs; it was that pungent. The quality of presence by which we had always known each other—that distinctive stamp of joy and tenderness—surrounded and enveloped me. If one could imagine the inner, emotional color of our time together without the outer supporting structure—like a mold cut away to reveal the casting—that is how it was.

In one of Rafe's favorite stories in *Out of Africa,* Isak Dinesen tells of being fascinated one day by a beautiful snake, its skin glistening with subtle, variegated colors. She raved so much about that snakeskin that one of her house servants killed the snake, skinned it, and brought it to her. To her dismay that once glistening skin was now just dull and gray. For the beauty had lain in the quality of its aliveness—in the tincture, not in the physical skin.

Now imagine if by spiritual work it were possible to disentangle the tincture from its physical carrier in the reverse fashion—so that the physical carrier dropped away and the quality of aliveness remained. This, I believe, is a God's-eye view of the process of death. The tincture is then carried in the body of hope.

I experienced just a taste of it that afternoon on the deck, when for a moment the Stanley place and all its artifacts dropped away and I could see the love itself and Rafe standing in the midst of it. The moment was fleeting, but it lasted long enough to light the path ahead.

Tincture is a recognition of things by their inner spiritual scent. Learning to do this is an acquired skill, but a tremendously important one because—as again Kabir Helminski points out—"two stones cannot occupy the same place, but two fragrances can."[7] This realization, I believe, holds the key to meeting (and melding) in the body of hope.

Conscious Will

The other aspect of this personalized presence comes in encountering Rafe's individual will. Hermeticists sometimes refer to a deceased person's psychic residues, but I am not speaking of this. By *psychic residues* they mean the subtle remains of the person's animating energies—emotions, memories, talents, and so on—which may vibrate intensely for a while following physical death, but have no real life of their own. I encounter Rafe's psychic residues in spades at his two dwelling places, the cabin and his grave, where all communication between us is intensified and magnified a hundredfold. But I am speaking of meeting an ongoing will, different from my own, and capable of lively and pointed interaction. There is definitely a real being there.

Again, my formative experience of this was at the funeral

wake. As I stood beside Rafe, it was as if a small spark of his will leaped from his being to mine, and I knew we were there "for the duration."

Since then, it has happened again several times, and I have found myself in the presence of a clear, resonant will different from my own. The most striking occurred on a beach in British Columbia in the fall of 1996, not quite a year after Rafe's death. I was spending several days in a teaching residency at Vancouver School of Theology. It was at the end of a hectic fall of teaching and workshops, and the time away from Colorado was beginning to wear on me. I felt homesick and drained, as if the very thing I was lecturing on—contemplative solitude—was slipping through my fingers. Sad and lonely, I went for a walk along the shore. I sat down on a jetty and stared out to sea, feeling like a duck out of water.

A sudden cat's-paw came hurtling across the water, and I knew something was about to happen. The first thing I heard was Rafe's voice, out of nowhere (not an audible voice, but a strong inner impression), laughing: "I love to see the water through you!" And then, to the heart of the matter: "You don't have to come all the way to me, because I am also coming to you." I could almost see the classic flounce of his head as he added his final tidbit, poignantly familiar: "You won't *let* me love you!"

It was true. My mistake was obvious. In my despairing sense that he was at rest, or on to higher spiritual things, I had figured that the burden of maintaining contact had fallen on me, and that I could only do it through intense prayer and solitude. It had never occurred to me that the very stranglehold of my efforts might be crowding out the space he needed simply to be present in my life. Somehow it had never dawned on me—at least in that way—that he cared.

It was an amazing psychological windshift, apparently out of nowhere. A moment before I had felt alone, homesick, caught in nostalgia. I got up from the jetty free and dancing.

Skeptics might dismiss the episode as pure fabrication. But I am inclined to trust in these visitations simply because of that bracing sense of an objectively "other" will coming up against my own and bending me in a direction quite different from my own natural inclinations. I do not think I would have come up with this revelation on my own. And even if I had, I have never once in all my years of psyching myself into things been able *from within myself* to produce such a unanimity of emotion around a new possibility. This encounter, I am convinced, came from outside me and not within me. And it had Rafe's stamp all over it.

THE BOOK OF LIFE

Along with energy, tincture, and conscious will, perhaps the most striking gift accessible within the body of hope is the potential for an open "book of life" between oneself and one's beloved—a mutual access to the sum total of their earthly impressions and memories, whether or not these experiences were actually shared in human life. In times of deep stillness and inner recollection, I find that pieces of Rafe's life lie open before me, almost as if we share a joint unconscious.

This is not as weird as it may sound. Governing it is a fairly simple principle that derives directly from the point just made: that after death, our tincture—the quality of our aliveness—is carried in the body of hope. And this quality of our aliveness, remember, is not some denatured extract of ourself; it is *the whole of our life*—all we have felt and dreamed and experienced and cared for—present in an infinitely more concentrated form.

Perhaps a simple analogy will help. One Sunday many years ago when I was still living in Maine, I put my daughter Lucy on the ferry from our island to the mainland four miles away to meet her boyfriend, Scott. Standing on a high bluff overlooking the bay on an exceptionally clear afternoon, I could watch the whole little drama play out. I saw each of the sequences unfolding in its turn: the ferry approaching the dock, Scott's car winding down the landing road. I could feel their rising excitements about the long-awaited rendezvous that was finally almost upon them. But from my vantage point, it was all present already, all contained in a huge stately "now." The dimension that for them was being lived in time, for me had been converted to space, and the picture was complete.

I believe something like this happens in the moment of death. The linearity that we experience in life as passing time becomes converted at the moment of death into a total presence to all that our life has been. This is why so many accounts of near-death experiences include the phenomenon of one's life flashing before one's eyes. In actual death, this flash does not then subside, but is already the beginning of a new dimension of oneself in the body of hope— what the Roman Catholic theologian Ladislaus Boros calls being "pancosmically present" to one's life. It is as if the wave that was our life now assumes particle form; it is present as one concentrated point. This may be what Nicoll was driving at when he said, "The soul is the image of the life." The soul is that larger picture—like me watching the ferry drama from the high hill—which contains the movements, the hopes, the animations, of life itself, all vividly and precisely preserved. And in this sense, then, we can indeed say that the *soul* is preserved in the body of hope.

This opens up enormous possibilities for continued growth and healing between partners whose love for each other unlocks the common book of their lives. For if those memories and experiences are all there and whole, preserved in the body of hope, they are also accessible—passing back into wave form, as it were—in the quiet heart of the deeply attuned beloved.

I remember the first time this happened to me and the extraordinary impact it created. As I mentioned earlier, I was not present at Rafe's death. He died alone in the monastery washroom, and it was several hours before anyone found him. More than anything else about his death, it was the hard piece to accept. Had he been frightened? Did he know what was happening to him? Did he rise to the sacrament of his death? Sadly, I had consigned all this to an ache I could never resolve—after all, I had not been there.

Up at the cabin on the first anniversary of his death, I had gone to bed early with no expectations of what the night would bring. About five minutes before the time of his death I came wide awake to find that I was actually reliving the last moments of his life—or more, being walked through them by a firm but tender presence. I was given to know that shortly before his heart finally burst, Rafe recognized the situation he was in and began reciting the Lord's Prayer, the prayer that for forty years had been the mainstay of his devotional life. In a way we have devised between ourselves to communicate when the human words themselves are of utmost importance, he moved in my jaw to form the words—"Our...Fa... ther...who...art...in...hea...ven"—as we rewalked together those last few inches of his human turf. The last words he said himself were "Thy will be done on earth as it is in heaven." On the "Give us this day our daily bread," his soul passed from life, and Rafe was carried across.

Again, skeptics can make the accusation here of colossal subjectivity. I am helpless to argue against it. All I know is that my heart filled with an assurance and joy as certain as if I had been there myself, and the lack of closure around his death has never again been an issue.

Like all psychic gifts, this one can certainly be abused. A willful conjuring up of the souls of the dead is known as necromancy and can cause grave spiritual harm. But fear of the misuse of the gift should not lead one to say that the gift does not exist. In the bond between partners who have loved deeply, the love itself is the safeguard, for the beloved will give, out of his or her own free will, what is needed for the other's becoming. One has only to open one's heart, in confidence, to that love itself, and what is truly necessary will come to pass.

CONFIGURATION

I should perhaps say a brief word about the forms in which the dead appear to us once they have left the physical body. With that strong visual orientation that seems to be our dominant sense in life, we naturally expect visions and full-body apparitions, and sometimes these do occur. I know friends who have had vivid apparitions of their partners—fully there with them in the room, clothed and realistic in every detail. This has never happened to me. The closest I have come to "seeing" Rafe—not counting occasional vivid dreams—is a gathering and intensification of that same golden light that was present in the church the night of the funeral wake. And sometimes, frankly, it is hard not to be disappointed. There are times when more than anything else I wish that he would suddenly appear, standing there beside me in the monastery communion circle, just like old times—just like Christ appearing to Mary Magdalene in the garden that Easter morning. Something inside us—or at least, inside me—seems to insist that the more vividly the beloved appears to your senses, the more deeply you are loved.

But the truth appears to be closer to the opposite. The operative principle governing apparitions is well demonstrated in the Gospels during those forty days of Jesus' resurrection appearances. Mary Magdalene, distraught in the garden, needs to see her beloved once again in human flesh. She does. But once she has seen him, her faith is satisfied; she believes and can move beyond despair without needing to touch. Thomas, who doubts strongly, is presented with a fully visceral humanity; he is invited not only to see, but to touch the wounds. He does, and he believes. And John, the "beloved disciple," has a faith so serene that he needs no private resurrection appearance; already he feels his risen Lord present in his heart. The principle seems to be that Jesus is physically present in precisely the degree needed to meet and fill the lack in the believer, that there may be an increase in "faith, hope, and love."

Thus, the particular form and nature of the appearance is really more governed by the needs of the still-embodied beloved than by the vibrancy of the one beyond flesh. With Rafe and me, the most common form of communion is through touch. Most often I will know he is there by the sense of an enfolding and encircling presence, often a distinct pressure. And I meet him also through words, which ring in my heart—as that day on the beach in British Columbia—but sometimes manifest themselves more outwardly as well. That "I love you" I so longed to hear in life has been heard many times since his death, fashioned just like on that night when I relived his death, by forming the words distinctly and powerfully in my jaw.

All of this is quite possible if one grasps the basic principle of the body of hope. One of the great conundrums that Christian theology has never fully resolved is whether we have a resurrection body—an individualized, permanent, noncorruptible flesh that becomes our permanent eternal identity. My growing suspicion is that our tincture—the core, essential quality of our aliveness, the whole of our life—is our resurrection body. It is carried whole and perfect in the body of hope, and depending upon its mobility—the degree of conscious self-configuration it has developed in this life through dedicated spiritual practice—that tincture has the ability to express itself in whatever way is appropriate to the human situation at hand.

ANAMNESIS

During the prayer of consecration in the Eucharist the words are spoken that Jesus himself used at the Last Supper: "Do this in remembrance of me." The early Christian Church was very clear in characterizing this remembrance as *anamnesis,* or "living presence." It was not a memorial of an event that had taken place in the past, or even a ritual repetition of it, but an actual making present of the risen Christ among the fellowship of believers. It was in a real sense a reunion with the living Christ that took place on the other side of death, through the holy elements of bread and wine.

The same word can be exactly applied to the body of hope. Living presence is what the body of hope is all about. It is the invitation to a continuously renewed immediacy with a person who is actually there, a reencounter that is always fresh and unpredictable.

When a person you love dies, it seems as though memory is all that is left. And memory itself fades or gets ripped away. In the few years since Rafe's death, almost all the little monuments to his existence have been erased. The Stanley place is a trash pile. The old Scout got sold for parts. Another monk is occupying the cabin, and still another has taken over the shop and cleared out the remains of Rafe's junk. Steadily his footprints recede from the earth, and trying to stay connected with him along that path is doomed.

But the other possibility exists—of making the leap to a direct and ongoing sharing of hearts and lives in the body of hope. Death does not have to mean the end of relationship and the slow receding of love. Henri Nouwen wrote shortly before his own death, "When one has loved deeply, that love can actually grow stronger after death." To discover how this is actually so is the fascinating and miraculous invitation open in this life to those who have loved deeply and are willing to keep walking toward that love.

CHAPTER II

BUILDING

SECOND BODY

It's a struggle all the way.

RAPHAEL ROBIN

THE BODY OF HOPE IS UNIVERSAL. But what is not universal is our conscious connection to it. Something must be formed in us that is able to receive and give, draw life and share it, within the body of hope. This something does not come naturally to us, but it is both possible and fitting for a human being to attain it. Indeed, many schools of inner transformation claim that this is specifically the purpose for which human beings were placed on this planet, because by the very process through which we acquire second body we also participate in the great intercirculation of higher energies—faith, hope, and love—that sustains conscious life on earth. In one form or another this establishing of our permanent, conscious connection to the body of hope is the goal of all inner spiritual work. In the Christian tradition it is known variously as developing "second body," "putting on the body of Christ," or receiving one's "wedding garment."

When it comes to soulwork beyond the grave, second body is indispensable. For as we saw in the last chapter, the field of unity that holds together two souls separated by death is the body of hope. Only there can the two beloveds encounter each other afresh, not in memory or psychic residue, but in the living presence of anamnesis, which allows their mutual becoming in love to continue unfolding. The real interchanges between them—of conscious will, energy, and their common book of life—will take place within the body of hope, and to work together, the partners must deal in that dimension. Without such a connection, I believe, the usual scenario holds sway: that slowly widening drift between the worlds.

FORMING SECOND BODY

In general, second body is formed in a person by going against the grain of life. All spiritual traditions speak of this, although in widely varied terminology that is easily misconstrued as pointless asceticism or renunciation of the world. Jesus' counsel that "whoever would save his life will lose it and whoever would lose it will save it" and the Desert Fathers' constant urgings to "beware the peace which comes from the flesh" are rooted in a common principle, which in fact is not a moral principle at all but an energetic one. In veiled and paradoxical language, this teaching points us toward the key to acquiring second body—namely, learning how to draw energy not from our usual physical and psychological processes (the *bios* that Valentin Tomberg refers to), but directly from *Zoe*, the living water of Life itself.

In natural human life, we draw our energy mainly through the ego, although most of us are probably unaware of this. We head into life with our needs, expectations, and desires, based on our inner image of who we are. As these hopes and needs are fulfilled, we experience enlivenment, that sense of well-being that comes when our lives feel worthwhile. This is "the peace that comes from the flesh." When our needs are frustrated, our expectations dashed or our passions triggered, our energy is squandered in emotional reactions. This happens to all of us. Sometimes it happens dozens of times a day.

The egoic process comes naturally to us, and it is in this sense that second body is formed in us by going against the grain of life. As long as we allow our energy to ebb and flow in us through the mechanical tide cycles of emotional reactivity, no deeper reservoir of spiritual attentiveness can begin to collect in us—the stuff out of which second body is made. The ruthless circularity of the egoic level seems designed to keep us squarely under the law of entropy, cruising along just beneath the critical velocity needed to leap into the next orbit (known in the Christian tradition as "faith") where we are finally able to move beyond "the peace that comes from the flesh" and step out into the desert to receive our bread from heaven.

According to Orthodox tradition, the real problem with all these emotional reactions is that they "divide our heart in two."[1] The heart divided cannot rise to its real task. For the heart—and the heart alone—is capable of drawing energy directly from *Zoe*.

Hence, the core of all spiritual practice lies in teaching us not to identify with our psychological reactions to everything. Depending on the path—Buddhism, Vedanta, the Christian inner tradition, Sufism—the language for the practice will vary. The Sufis call it "dying before you die"—a phrase that obviously resonates deeply with Jesus' own "whoever would lose his life will save it." But whatever the language, the underlying principle is the same: if we can stop living exclusively according to our likes and dislikes, drawing and then squandering our energy through egoic reactions, then something finer will begin to gather in us that allows us even here and now to participate in the more subtle vibrations of divine life.

HOW RAFE DID IT

Since this may all sound rather abstract, perhaps the best thing is to ground it in Rafe's own story.

Rafe was on the trail of second body from early on, although he didn't know it at first. Even before he entered the monastery, while he was still absorbing the first shock waves of a profound religious conversion at his brother's farm in Mississippi, he had come upon a quote in a newspaper: "Happy the man who realizes that his happiness does not rely on anything outside himself." From the start that quote galvanized Rafe. He sensed in it a kind of inner independence that haunted him—and also left him a bit restless in the highly regimented structure of conventional monasticism. He hung in for eighteen years as a Trappist lay brother, but it bothered him more and more that the lifestyle seemed to allow people to slip by, simply going through the motions. "They spend all their time going up and down the steps," he complained of his fellow monks, who seemed to see no more to the process of spiritual transformation than simply putting in their hours tramping up and down the staircase to the daily round of prayer services in the old pine-board chapel. Finally he won permission to join an experimental Trappist community in North Carolina, where he bumped into a copy of P. D. Ouspensky's *In Search of the Miraculous* and could at last begin to put a name to that elusive quality he had been seeking for so long. Later, after he arrived in Colorado, someone gave him the five-volume set of Nicoll's *Psychological Commentaries on the Teaching of Gurdjieff and Ouspensky,* which he read from every day, along with his Bible; these became the twin cornerstones of his spiritual work.

By the time I met him, some twenty years later, he had developed a largely self-taught Fourth Way practice that he called "shifting gears smoothly"—a way of making a smooth connection between the deep stillness of contemplative prayer and the manual work by which he earned his keep. A lot of people who saw Rafe's collection of old snowmobiles and constantly broken-down junk assumed he was either eccentric or cheap. In fact, he deliberately used the work with machines—a craft he admittedly hated and had no natural aptitude for—as a tool for seeing and working on himself, observing his emotional reactions and moving beyond them. Even in the midst of trying conditions and his ongoing struggle with an explosive temper, there was a person there who was constantly watching, measuring, and exploring. Pinned up on the wall of the shop was a quote from Nicoll that pretty much summed up his practice:

> Faith is a continual inner effort, a continual altering of the
> mind, of the habitual ways of thought, of the habitual ways of
> taking everything, of habitual reactions...[2]

When I came into Rafe's life, much of our work together was simply a matter of my joining him in his practice. It meant a lot of hours spent tinkering with snowmobiles or down in the pump house at the Stanley place as I worked along with him and learned an attitude about work and a way of working on oneself. People sometimes ask me what our spiritual practice was; it was basically that. In the friction of the work itself—and often in the friction of each other—we had to step back, get a second wind, and reorient ourselves around the higher purposes we both claimed we were striving toward. I had worked in Fourth Way groups before I met Rafe, but never have I worked with anyone, either before or since, who could apply the Work principles with such consistency and ferocity of purpose.[3]

I remember vividly an episode less than two weeks before his death. The driveshaft had dropped out of the Scout. It turned out, once we'd gotten it up on blocks in the monastery garage, that the frame had been bent in that nightmare ride down the hill when Rafe had passed out at the wheel and wound up sideways in a ditch.

Anyone else would have given up on the old Scout, but not Rafe. Clambering underneath with hammer, crowbar, and arc welder—mostly lying on his back in a pool of water as the frozen mud on the undercarriage gradually thawed out—he patched the frame, then slowly started to reassemble the driveshaft from the pile of worn and greasy parts at his side. At one point toward the end of the ordeal, when a particularly stubborn gasket refused to yield to either friendly persuasion or brute force, hammer and screwdriver came flying out from beneath the Scout, followed by an impressively unmonastic string of profanity. I started to rescue the hammer, but as I grabbed for it, out from underneath the Scout wriggled two muddy boots. With icy dignity Rafe walked over, picked up the hammer, and stood there holding it, shaking with exhaustion and rage, eyes tight shut. Slowly the shaking subsided. When his eyes opened again, they shone with that fierce, faraway blue that seemed to emanate from a point far beyond life.

"Rafe, I don't know why you don't quit," I said.

"Neither do I."

By the end of the day the old Scout was back on the road. It would carry him up and down the hill for one more trip before death relieved them both of their struggle.

That was the flavor of Rafe's own work. There was nothing mystical or elegant about it. It was brutal, step-by-step trying in every moment to stay awake, to move beyond the habitual, to see. There in the mud and grease of ordinary life Rafe carved his path to liberation. As Jacob Boehme said of his own struggle into spiritual emergence: "But what I am, that all men are who wrestle in

Jesus Christ our King for the crown of eternal joy, and live in the hope of perfection."[4]

SELF-CONFIGURATION

The purpose of such spiritual work is not penance or martyrdom. What begins to gather in a person—by conscious seeing—is a certain inner independence from the external conditions of one's life. Maurice Nicoll says simply and directly, "The man who has reached a stage in which he has something independent of failure and success, cold or heat, comfort or discomfort, starvation or plenty, such a man has Second Body."[5] And Valentin Tomberg defines this second body as "an etheric body independent of the life forces that can draw its energy directly from the Spiritual life world."[6]

In both these definitions, I see the same touchstone: independence. This second body is independent of the chain reactivity that characterizes life at the psychological level. A man or woman who has acquired second body has indeed come to "realize that happiness does not depend on anything outside." Discovering and uniting with something deeper within that endures beneath the psychological storms, such a person begins to acquire a freedom that some writers call "permanent individuality." Even on a freezing, muddy garage floor with a job somewhere between impossible and hopeless, one can still find that invincible inner point.

Ladislaus Boros describes the process of forming second body as well as I have seen it described anywhere in esoteric literature— emphasizing also that it is "the supremely individual creation of a man." In a significant passage in *The Mystery of Death* he writes:

> From the facts of experience and the surrounding world an
> inner sphere of being a human being is built up. This inner
> man is brought about by a never-ending application on the

treadmill of duties, annoyances, joys and difficulties. From these insignificant actions freely performed, the great decisive freedom is built up—freedom from oneself, freedom to view one's own existence from the outside.[7]

Please note an important nuance in what Boros is saying here: these actions must be "freely performed"—i.e., with an attention that is not totally bound up and caught in the activities themselves. It is not merely a matter of putting in one's hours on the daily treadmill of duties that brings about this inner self, but rather, developing a conscious relationship to the material of one's life. As Rafe knew full well, there was nothing intrinsically holy about a lifetime spent mending broken snowmobiles—nor, for that matter, a lifetime spent in the mechanical repetition of prayers and daily office. What matters above all is that conscious relationship—that capacity for seeing and reflecting and standing slightly apart from one's existence. It is the material of daily life, passed through the mirror of reflective consciousness, that begins to create second body—or "being," as Boros calls it. He continues:

The external freedom of action diminishes as time passes, as the vital forces slowly but inexorably fail. At last man appears in the fullness of his days and works, and in the inestimable possession of a definitively achieved deliverance. From the crowded days and years of joy and sorrow something has crystallized out, the rudimentary forms of which were already present in all his experiences, his struggles, his creative work, his patience and love—namely, the inner self, the supremely individual creation of a man. He has given his own shape to the determinisms of life by a daily conquest of them; he has become the master of the multiple relations that go to make him up by accepting them as the raw material of his self. Now he begins to "be."[8]

Quite strikingly—considering that this is a Roman Catholic theologian speaking—Boros further notes that one of the attributes of the inner man fully realized is that he configure himself— "he can call into existence out of the bases of his own being a body (no less) and a relationship with his surroundings and his neighbors."[9] For such a man, death is not an end, but an extension of this tendency already visibly under way in life. It is the state in which "he can produce a corporeity of his own and so be free—self-posited, right down to the most hidden fibres of his reality."[10]

This insight is both brilliant and astonishing. The starting point is in the psychological realm; the end point is in the physical. What begins as a psychological self-configuration—an interior capacity to reflect and "recompose" oneself as Rafe did that day at the garage—gradually emerges into an actual physical capacity to "produce a corporeity of one's own"—to move and act from beyond life itself, in the body of hope.

Boros equates this transition point with the moment of death, but from my work with Rafe I suspect that the transition begins far earlier and more gradually for dedicated spiritual practitioners. By the time I met him, Rafe was already fairly adept at "producing a corporeity for himself" beyond the physical body—that's what the "everything that can be had in a hug is already here" lesson was all about—and in the last weeks of his life, this aspect of his relationship with himself became strikingly pronounced. Overall, his physical vitality was clearly waning. But at times he seemed to draw surges of life out of nowhere, and the whole shape of his body would change almost before my eyes. I am not talking about an old man trying to act young or being momentarily swept up in my own vitality, but something much more deliberate and conscious. During our last conversation, I had the distinct impression that he had taken himself back to a man in his late forties, my age, and was holding himself there by sheer force of will, as if he wanted me to meet that person in physical life, remember him as that person when death separated our physical bodies. Months later, when an old photograph happened to come my way of Rafe, age forty-eight, standing outside his little cabin at Waunita Hot Springs, Colorado, I nearly fell over in disbelief. I was staring once again at the very face I had last looked upon in physical life.

This ability to physically configure oneself by conscious will is by no means a psychic phenomenon, but rather, I believe, a normal inner progression as one approaches spiritual eldership, a sign that the process of acquiring second body is well advanced. It speaks of a growing detachment of the tincture, or quality of one's aliveness, from its basis in the physical body. In ordinary life, the two are virtually inseparable; in fact, according to some hermetic schools, it is the specific function of the "vital body" to keep the quality of our aliveness inextricably pasted to our physical body until the moment of death. But as second body begins to grow in us, it more and more carries the tincture, and since it draws its sustenance directly from *Zoe*, the eternal life energy, there is an increasing independence from the physical life energies themselves. Far from being dependent on the physical body, the liberated tincture can express itself directly without a body, or even, on occasion, reconfigure the body to suit its purpose. For a person well along on this path, as Rafe was, it can be understood how death will pose relatively little disruption to one's sense of identity or ability to act. It is merely doing for keeps what one has already been practicing.

I am convinced that a person who reaches the hour of death with no developed second body—no conscious relationship and shape to the material of his life—does, indeed, "rest" in the classic sense of Christian teaching. I am unwilling, by my own Christian roots, to take the view that Gurdjieff took by assuming such a soul is annihilated. But I believe that for the vast majority of souls the Church's explanation of rest is in fact true, until the final day of judgment, whatever one construes this to be. Boehme avers that most souls enter heaven "hanging as by a thread"[11]—"and these souls must wait till the last day for their bodies; they remain in their bodies in the still rest, till the last day, without feeling any pain but in another principle." Only those who through dedicated spiritual work in this life have crystallized second body within them will have the means in the kingdom beyond death to act—to participate as conscious servants in the unfolding of divine love, both in this world and in the world beyond. From the standpoint of life beyond the grave, second body confers the all-important capacity of mobility.

The Sufi master Hazrat Inayat Khan expressed this same point in a picturesque way: "Those who are given liberty by Him to act freely are nailed on the earth, and those who are free to act as they choose on the earth will be nailed in the heavens."[12] There is a trade-off required—not bargaining, exactly, but a wager one must stake one's life on. Acquiring second body is no fun and requires hard and dedicated work—in Rafe's words, "It's a struggle all the way." Far easier to coast along on the enchantments and diversions of life, the ready-made explanations of who one is and what one's life means. It may also mean sacrificing a lot of potential growth at the horizontal level, like a plant that must be pruned in order to bear fruit. This is what is meant by being "nailed on the earth." If one does not believe in the fruit, then the pruning will always seem like a folly.

CHAPTER 12

RAFE AFTER DEATH

"A MAN WITHOUT A BODY is infinitely more alive than a man with a body."

So my friend Murat Yagan told me, when I visited him in his spiritual community in British Columbia. Murat, eighty years old himself and well accustomed to intercommunion with the spiritual realm, spoke with the absolute matter-of-fact veracity that left me double-taking.

It *is* hard to believe. Partially, I believe, because of that extreme credibility barrier posed by death itself. Inevitably, death comes as the end of a gradual or swift physical decline; it is the waning of energies, the passing into physical decrepitude. And then there is only the body itself, vacant and lifeless, an apparent caricature of all that the person was. When I first encountered Rafe at the funeral wake, there was that inevitable initial "frisson": the one who only a few days before had been so alive, blue eyes flashing, was now locked up tightly in the mask of death, gray and unmoving. Only when I became still enough to catch his presence at a more subtle level was I able to move through that mask to the remarkable reunion that lay beyond it.

And so I have learned it is true in Rafe's case—"a man without a body is infinitely more alive than one with a body." Not only that, but it is *his* aliveness, large enough for both of us, that principally spurs and sustains my own quest.

The fifth-century desert father and spiritual master John Cassian wrote at length about the soul beyond death. It is an interesting passage (the bulk of his First Conference), and worth quoting at length, since it constitutes the most powerful statement I have found within Christian tradition of the position that after death the soul does not merely "rest in the hope of rising again" (the usual teaching), but lives far more intensely and responsively. Cassian begins his teaching by reflecting on the parable (in Luke 16) of the rich man clothed in purple and the poor man Lazarus, who both die and awake to find that the circumstances have been reversed; the rich man is in Hades, while Lazarus is in paradise. It is not this reversal that interests Cassian, however, but a more subtle point:

> The gospel parable of the poor man Lazarus and of the rich man clothed in purple show us that souls separated from the body are neither inactive nor bereft of feeling. The one man wins as his blessed abode the peace that exists in the bosom of Abraham; the other is subjected to the unbearable scorchings of eternal fire. And if we wish to ponder what was said to the thief, namely, "Today you shall be with me in paradise," what other obvious meaning is there to this if not that souls continue to have their former sense of awareness and, further, that their lot is in keeping with their merits and with what they have done? The Lord would never have made this promise to the thief if he knew that the soul, once separated from the body, must lose all feeling and be turned into noth-

ing. For it was the soul and not the body which would go with Christ to paradise....

All of this clearly shows that not only are the souls of the dead not deprived of their intellectual faculties but that they also are not lacking in feelings such as hope and sadness, joy and fear. They already have a foretaste of what is in store for them after the general judgment. Nor does it happen, as some unbelievers would hold, that upon leaving this world they are turned to nothing. Actually, they live more intensely and they concentrate more on the praises of God....

[If we are truly made in the image and likeness of God, then] it must surely follow, it must certainly happen that when the mind has shed the inhibiting grossness of the flesh it recovers in improved form its intellectual capacities, that it gathers, not loses, these in a purer and more penetrating condition.[1]

"Actually, they live more intensely..." As Cassian pictures it, the soul beyond death is not devoid of responsiveness—"hope and sadness, joy and fear"—but these feelings are heightened and clarified in the mirror of truth held out by death itself.

My own first experience of having been set down on very different relational ground came not long after the funeral, up at Rafe's cabin. I was still numb with grief, and my impulse was to remember Rafe, to keep him alive by a redoubled effort to live what he had lived, to take upon myself his hermit striving. "It's a work," he had always said of the hermit life, "but someone's got to do it." It now seemed inevitable that that someone was *me*, and I had come up to the cabin to give myself as deeply as I could to this new post.

Instead, to my astonishment, at the end of an intense morning of prayer, I found myself writing in my journal, the pen literally streaming out in front of me:

> Right here at the end, out of my tears, you [Rafe] handed me an astonishing gift, as you always do. You speak in my heart and say—
>
> "Don't strain so. Don't cling. Don't use your energies to force the connection. I will not forget you. Let me hold you in my heart; that is the office more proper to one gone beyond the body. Relax and trust me, and let yourself be loved.
>
> "You may not have to do the post. For I did it for both of us. What was done was done for both of us.
>
> "Rather, the gift I would make to you—giving and receiving one—is that you simply live your life with all the joy, fullness, healing, and abundance that is my gift to you in love. Don't copy me, don't cling to me, don't carry my oar anywhere and plant it. But find and plant your own oar, knowing that of all things that is the wildest, the freest, and will give me great joy.
>
> "You will see that it exists. Always. Unrescindable. Not going away.
>
> "Take up your life and live it. And I will be there in the midst of it. There in your heart.
>
> "Live your life as the gift it is."

It was an astonishing moment, out of nowhere, but utterly clear and resonant with its own vibrancy. I have had recurrent reminders of that message—that afternoon on the beach in British Columbia was another of them, and there have been many others as well. Once early on, as I was struggling to sort out in my mind the confusing and sketchy details of his life, I suddenly heard him say, "Quit it! It's useless to rummage about in my life. Who I was in life was incomplete. Instead, accept who I am now—what I am growing into."

And what is that? Toward the end of his life, Rafe copied out several lines from a poem by D. H. Lawrence:

And if, in the changing phases of man's life
I fall in sickness and in misery
my wrists seem broken and my heart seems dead
and strength is gone, and my life is only the
*   leavings of a life:*

and still, among it all, snatches of lovely oblivion
*   and snatches of renewal*
odd, wintry flowers upon the withered stem, yet
*   new, strange flowers*
such as my life has not brought forth before, new
*   blossoms of me—*

then I must know that still
I am in the hands of the unknown God,
he is breaking me down to his new oblivion
to send me forth on a new morning, a new man.[2]

That was Rafe in a nutshell. The Rafe before death who was, particularly in those last weeks, after our wrestling match, beginning to blossom before my eyes: loving and nurturing, at ease with himself, utterly radiant in his gratitude for life, his joy in God. Dancing along with the unknown God, marveling at the "new, strange blossoms of himself," the emergence of human love: that one, Rafe says, is the one to encounter, receive, in the walk beyond death. Could it be, I wondered, that Rafe had to die out of his hermit post to accept what he truly was, the "pure becoming" in love? Like the blade of grain fully ripe, he cracked the husk.

THE MOMENT OF DEATH

Confirmation of this growing inkling came to me from an unexpected quarter. I was up at the cabin one afternoon sorting through
Rafe's books when there, poking out from the shelves, was a copy
of Ladislaus Boros's *The Mystery of Death*. I pulled it out with a
start, recognizing a long-forgotten friend. I recalled having
devoured it some twenty years earlier, soaking up whole paragraphs
by memory, which came back to me in force as I flipped through
the pages once again—but I'd never realized till that moment that
Rafe knew the book, too! It was another of those unspoken connecting links between us. Reading it again, eight months after his
death, was not only a profound déjà vu but also a substantial help
in putting chapter and verse to my growing sense that death had
released Rafe into such a new ballpark of freedom and wholeness
that the old Rafe was, in some ways, virtually immaterial.

I have already drawn extensively on Boros in my earlier discussion of second body, but would like to return once again to this brilliant but curiously little known work—which was written, I gather,
virtually straight through in a white heat of illumination and bears
the earmarks of such works of revealed truth in the boldness of its
leaps and the strange authority of its presentation. In his fascinating hypothesis of death as "a convergence upon a moment of final
decision" (made not by God but by ourselves), Boros claims that
death gives us the opportunity to make our first completely free and
personal act; far from bringing annihilation, it is the moment more
than any other for the awakening of consciousness and freedom.

The moment has been in preparation from a long way off. As
the body ages, our physical vitality inevitably declines, but our inner
life is all the while growing proportionately wide and vast; and the
opportunity is there—if, as we saw in the last chapter, we have the

courage to accept it—to learn to configure ourselves with an increasing independence from our physical corporeity. At last, in death, the physical body drops away altogether, and in this moment the soul in total "ontological exposure"[3]—cut loose for the first time from its physical matrix—comes fully into sight of itself. It is a moment of sudden total awakening to ourselves. "Everything we have ever guessed at, sensed, and loved," Boros claims, in a single moment is before us, as we are totally present to ourself, to the world, and to Christ.[4] We are who we are in bare essence, but that which we are, we *are*, fully and completely self-expressive. And in this instant of awakening, says Boros, we make our "first completely personal act"—the decision for or against God, which is really none other than the decision to accept or reject the divine love flooding over and through us.

"Don't you see how changeable I am?" Rafe had fretted that brutally honest night between us at the cabin. Boros takes Rafe's anguished self-observation to its implicit conclusion when he claims that the major impediment to attaining unity of being here in life is the body itself—this "temple of myself" that can only do, experience, and express one thing at a time, and that sees everything as an extension of itself, and hence of its own self-interest. "Existence is inseparable from its embodiment"[5]; that is the problem—particularly when one is trying to give oneself fully in love. The limitation of corporeity itself is what creates the inevitable, variegated dimensions of our selfhood, like cut glass. We can only be one facet at a time, one slice of ourselves, one expression. Many different personalities clamor within us, and while our inner work can bring about a certain progress toward mastering one's household, it would appear that this kaleidoscope of moods, poses, and self-images, each one with its own assertive energy, is the lump sum of who we humanly are. Toward the end, like a dying fire, different embers of Rafe would flare up, flicker brilliantly: the impassioned beloved, the striving hermit, the struggling old man...flicker and then die. And yet the essential self remains always in some sense hidden—"with Christ in God," the monks like to say. Planetary existence does not seem to yield the vastness of conditions to fully bear and manifest who we are. It bursts forth for a glimpse only in those transfigured moments when we are shined through...or wept through.

At the moment of death, it would seem that who we are—the full moon behind the sliver, the underlying unity of our being, which we have longed for and somehow known all along was there—is now able to step forth and express itself. Says Boros: "The personal element in all its fullness—in other words, the inner man—can only emerge in death, when the energies of the outer man disappear."[6] What is finally revealed behind these outer energies may be tiny indeed; only a dot. But it is our coherent organizing principle, for within it is contained our complete authenticity, the unity of our being. And it is that dot which now passes over— or glows fully—in death, bearing, like the bush that burns but is not consumed, the core disposition of the soul.

Jacob Boehme, you recall, also describes this moment of death in terms of fire and light. After earlier stating that "God wills and works in...the resigned will, by which the soul is made holy and comes to divine rest," Boehme goes on to envision the moment of death for such a soul as pure incandescent light: "When the body breaks up, the soul is pressed through with divine love and is illuminated with God's light as fire glows through iron by which it loses its darkness."[7] Death becomes the template for the soul: the moment in which the soul's true form is eternally revealed in the light of divine love.

Whatever this form may be—and I will have more to say on the matter in chapter 14—the moment of our death releases us, finally, to the full depths of our human love. As Boros says: "Our first possibility of acting out our love fully is given us in the moment of death when our whole existence is exposed and surrendered. This ontological exposure (death) gives us the space we need for a decision of self-surrender (love)."[8] With nothing any more to hold back or protect, love, the life of our soul, is free to pour out in full measure. For me, that was the extraordinary grace of our encounter that night of Rafe's funeral wake. For the first time, he was completely, consistently open to the force of his own love. And that has continued to be the chief measure of our new way of being together.

I cannot say that I buy Boros's entire argument. His stipulation that the moment of death is a final decision beyond which no alteration is possible is obviously incompatible with my own experience of mutual growth beyond death, and I believe it rests on a common theological misassumption (that growth is a function of time) that I will speak to in the next chapter. But on the whole, I have been enormously helped by his reminder that death is a sacred passage that brings about a qualitative and quantum change in being. Even for those spiritual adepts who have mastered the art of dying before you die, death is still its own unique gate; personhood on the other side of it will be different. It is not simply a matter of the body dropping off when it is no longer needed to sustain personal identity; the passage through death itself somehow mysteriously bestows that crucial final element of personal identity that can be acquired in no other way. I believe Christ's own death on the cross teaches this; it is a core and profound wisdom of the Christian path.

And so Rafe and I *are* in different places, and something definitively sacred has happened to him, which for me still lies ahead. I find this thought strangely comforting in those moments when, moved by self-pity, I want him back again in his body. The one who he is now, who is "infinitely more alive than he was in his body," is the fruit of that passage through death, and in my heart of hearts I would not have it any other way. What he could not do fully in life, he can do fully now, and that is part of the ongoing becoming between us that gives this time now its particular grace and freshness. And for myself, too, I trust and hope in that moment of my own passage, when, like Rafe, I will fall through the sliver into the full-of-the-moon.

At any rate, for me here on the human side of things, my most difficult challenge by far has been to let Rafe grow: to let him be fully expressive of who he is now rather than clinging to who he was; to "receive the growing Raphael," to paraphrase the contemporary mystic Bede Griffiths's final words.

It is difficult because I realize it flirts dangerously with the realm of pure subjectivity. At least *this* side the divide of Rafe's passing, I am accompanied by a small band of folks—some of the monks, a few of the ranchers—who knew with something approaching intimacy who Rafe was, what he stood for, what values animated his core. They knew him as a cowboy, a private, rough-hewn man, passionate about his solitude and about nature. To say that death has brought to light a different side of him— more urbane, more confident, artistic, and deeply nurturing—is to describe a Rafe that no one would recognize, and for which there is virtually no external confirmation. Even if I were to describe some of the last conversations we had—about Gregorian chant, objective art, Chartres cathedral; if I were to remark how under that exterior he was actually a very good poet and a fair composer—most would be hard put to believe it. And death has only intensified the movement in this direction.

Curiously, a scrap of empirical confirmation fell into my lap the summer after Rafe's death when a young woman, a composition student at the Aspen Music School, wound up camping out for a few weeks up at the cabin. She knew nothing of who Rafe was—not even his name; she just went about her thing, highly sensitively, living in the cabin and composing her music. Later that summer she even premiered a piece called "From a Monk's Cabin." When I talked to her about Rafe sometime afterward, she said, "I felt my composing was assisted. I felt that I was living in the presence of an artist, a man of great creativity." I found this fascinating, in that she is the first one I know to have met only the Rafe beyond death, with no prior reference points in the old Rafe.

My sense is that through love of the growing Rafe, I also am called to become an unknown person: a person who, like him, is somehow still unfolding along the trajectory of the time we spent together; to become the person I would have become if he were still here, if our life had had human duration—for he is, and it does. The fused whole greater than the sum of the parts—"the abler soul which thence doth flow," grasped by him in death and glimpsed by me when I surrender into his love—must henceforth be the pattern that orders both of our becomings. This is both the great challenge and the great grace of work together beyond the grave.

CHAPTER 13

DO THE DEAD GROW?

"RECEIVE THE GROWING RAPHAEL..." But are we really talking about growth here, or is it a metaphor? Beyond death can people still grow?

This is the "Holy Planet Purgatory" issue again, which seems to make Christian theologians so nervous. Even the best of them, such as Boehme and Boros, categorically deny the possibility. "After this life there will be no bettering, but everything remaineth as it returneth home," writes Boehme.[1] And Boros takes up the traditional doctrine of the inalterability of the state we reach through death: "A human existence that has passed through death has reached a final state in which no further change is possible in its basic tendency. At death a man's final figure with the destiny it deserves is irrevocably attributed to him. Once beyond death no more decisions altering the course of one's existence can be made....Death, therefore, is the dawn of finality. In it man receives his definite shape. Death transports existence to the realm of things 'valid for eternity,' to the state of 'done once and for all.'"[2]

This is the overwhelming tenor of our received Christian tradition of existence beyond death. Allowance is made that the prayers of the faithful can improve the state of those who have reached eternal life "hanging by a thread" (in Boehme's picturesque language)—the traditional notion of purgatory; but this has always been understood as a release from the debt of sin rather than an organic increase of personhood. Our fundamental understanding is that the dead rest—"in the hope of rising again"; our deepest prayer is for the "repose of their souls."

And yet in my heart of hearts I know this is not true. The Rafe I encounter beyond death—vibrant, opinionated, reveling in his newfound freedom—is definitely not at rest; he is surpassingly in movement. Our traditional Christian concepts of the state beyond death cannot possibly honor the quality of its aliveness, let alone the possibility of a reciprocal nurturance with the world here below.

Part of the problem is that our notion of growth, from our human perspective, is linked to linearity and progress (Boros's "existential set toward the future"); time is an essential dimension of growth. When "time is swallowed up in death," it is nearly impossible to visualize what growth might look like.

But starting from love rather than time, I understand something else: for growth is an essential quality of love—in fact, its innermost reality. Remember Beatrice Bruteau's powerful insight that love calls forth the reality of the beloved, and the act of loving calls forth one's own deepest reality. Love is precisely that which calls forth the continued emergence of the beloved, that guides into being the new life, the new potentiality. Love's nature is that it evokes an increase in being. Where there is love, there must be increase.

Moreover, as I have come to understand the nature of this particular path I am walking on, which some have called the Fifth Way, the love of the unique beloved, the distinctive quality of this love is the complete mutuality of giving and receiving. The desire to give all for the other is the essence of true romance, the heart of the alchemy that transforms desire into redemptive love. But this mutuality can be authentic only if the possibility truly exists that *my* gift means something—that it continues to call forth the reality of the beloved, to help Rafe grow. If the Law of Love takes precedence over the Law of Time—which I think is the inevitable implication of the statement "Love is stronger than death"—then we must affirm that growth of the beloved beyond the grave is somehow possible, even if we do not know what this means. In this chapter I want to begin to visualize what it might look like.

"MY GIFT TO YOU IN LOVE . . ."

The first inner clue that I was headed into completely uncharted waters came in this strange but persistent sense that Rafe did not want me to do the same thing he had done in his life—to take up the values he had stood for so passionately and live them out in my own remote hermitage. That came through so strongly even in his words to me that day at the cabin, barely two weeks after his death: "You may not have to do the post. For I did it for both of us.... Rather, the gift I would make to you...is that you simply live your life with all the joy, fullness, healing, and abundance that is my gift to you in love." It sounds almost silly to say it, but I felt that it pained him, in a way, to see me struggle so hard in all the ways he had struggled: chopping wood, fussing with cranky snowmobiles, getting splinters in my hands. Enough of this penitential mode! If the wedding feast had really happened that night, then I should be living like a bride!

And then came that reassurance on the beach at British Columbia: "You don't have to come all the way to me, because I am also coming to you." And in a way its even more telling aside: "I love to see the water through you!" I had to admit that despite the profound unitive solitude of the cabin, the times when I most keenly felt his presence—alive, excited, and vibrant with that joy that was so much the hallmark of our human sharing—were in those moments when I was preaching and teaching and embracing life with my own unique gifts and talents. The force of his will became stronger and stronger on this point, until finally it became impossible to swim upstream against it. Every time I would head up to the cabin to deepen solitude, at the center of it was always that same message: "Go; go back into the world. You don't have to do the post; I did it for both of us."

But why? That seemed to be the real issue. Was it for me—to let me off the hook, release me gently from partnership back into the life I had lived many years before? Or was it for *us*—in some enigmatic way not a release from partnership, but an even more profound commitment to it? The solution to this enigma, I sensed, also held the key to the "growth-beyond-death" koan.

And so what to make of it? Was this Rafe's way of gently nudging me loose from a lifestyle I had grabbed on to inauthentically under the influence of meeting him? I didn't think so. The tracks toward the hermit life had begun early in my life, some fifteen years before I ever met him, when I walked away from an academic career in Philadelphia in search of deeper solitude on a Maine island. It had been almost my oldest and truest inner voice and had been confirmed by many others along the way, as well as by Rafe himself. This new set of instructions did not feel like a release back into my old life, but a marked change in direction.

Nor did Rafe's words suggest a release from partnership. In fact, quite the opposite: "I did it for both of us"..."I am also coming to you"…"Take up your life and live it, and I will be there in the midst of it." It sounded like strong reassurance that the partnership was still intact—but that Rafe seemed to have some specific preferences as to how I lived out my half of it. I did not take his words to imply a general benevolent blessing on anything I wanted to do with my life, but rather a promise of specific support and help to do the one thing I had to do, which was to accept and live out a radically new destiny that was not just about me, but somehow involved both of us.

For that was the other, and wilder, possibility. What if it did, in fact, involve both of us? What if we were both being shaped to a whole new trajectory that had begun two and a half years earlier when we first collided in love? What if there was something needed, some food for the organic increase of his personhood beyond the grave, that was generated in the dynamics between us: in the way we loved, the way we worked, the way we called each other into being—and that I could continue to give simply by opening my life completely to it? If we could just keep the dance going between us—just keep following the course that our life would most likely have followed if it had unfolded in time—then somehow we would be doing it, and the "pure becoming" that had already been the pattern of our human love would continue to flesh itself out (even with one flesh gone!) in the body of hope.

For various reasons, I have come to accept this perhaps far-fetched hypothesis as the correct interpretation of the situation. If nothing else, it fulfills the "Love believes all things" stipulation of the 1 Corinthians 13 passage—St. Paul's famous hymn to love, which has become my own most trustworthy guide in this walk beyond the grave.[3] For it *is* the highest possibility that can be lived out in the situation, calling forth the deepest trust and the most

profound gift of self. "This act of total surrender is not merely a fan-
tastic intellectual and mystical gamble;" says Thomas Merton in a
passage that has helped me very much, "it is something much more
serious. It is an act of love for this unseen person who, in the very
gift of love by which we surrender ourselves to his reality also makes
himself present to us."[4] While Merton's "unseen person" is Christ,
his words describe precisely the dance between Rafe and myself,
with its subtle dynamics of total surrender in love somehow making present the becoming Reality. The reciprocity of this giving also
holds the key to the mystery of organic growth beyond the grave.

I have talked with a few of my closest spiritual friends, and not
one has been able to understand it. To lay down my own sense of
inner direction in order to allow a beloved to grow in a direction
that during life he consciously spurned seems like pure madness.
"You mean your hermit teacher is telling you not to be a hermit?" I
grit my teeth, but there it is.

For if what we really did was to bring into being an abler soul
between us, then we are both accountable to it, and I must obey and
trust even where I don't yet fully see. I do not have to repeat what
Rafe did here; instead, what I must accomplish is something he did
not do here; I must do it for both of us.

And it can only be done in the one dimension he now lacks and
I still have: time.

CHAPTER 14

ESSENCE AND

MAJESTY

IF THERE IS A SECRET to love's transforming power, surely it must lie in its uncanny ability to call forth who we truly are. "Love always seeks the ultimately *real*," says Bruteau; it has an infallible knack for pushing through dim outer shells and inner dark places and bringing the essence of who we are into the light. Love always brings about an increase in being, and it does so by giving us the courage and power to live out who we truly are. This is the simple and completely straightforward meaning of that fundamental esoteric doctrine: love actualizes essence.

With this reference point in mind, I want to pick up again where I left off in chapter 12, with Ladislaus Boros's scenario of what takes place in the moment of death, and my own earlier comments on that scenario. The moment of death, according to Boros, plunges the soul into "total ontological exposure," which is also, paradoxically, its first moment of complete, unanimous coherence. For the first time the whole picture is opened, ordered around its core principle, and held fully present to itself. The pretenses, the parts tied to the false self and the outer energies, disappear with the outer energies themselves. The parts that belong authentically to oneself but have not been fully actualized and integrated in life simply remain dark, like the full of the moon faintly present behind the sliver. And in this timeless instant, backlit against the light of divine love, the soul's true stature is revealed in two dimensions: *mobility* and *majesty*.

These two coordinates, mobility and majesty, are the indispensable starting points for approaching soulwork beyond the grave, for together they plot the graph of the soul's destiny. If you think of mobility as the vertical axis and majesty as the horizontal, you have a concrete way to pinpoint the position of the soul in its moment of death, and also to gauge the size of the essence territory it has been able to enclose during its earthly journey.

Mobility is the power of movement within the Kingdom of Heaven—"the liberty to act freely," as Hazrat Inayat Khan described it; it is the opposite of the rest generally attributed to the soul after death. In the classic spiritual traditions of the West, mobility is created by dying to self.

The other coordinate is majesty. The term comes from Boehme, and as we saw earlier, majesty is created through "the wonders thou hast wrought and found out here." Rather than dying to self, majesty is created by *awakening* to self, "playing out the hand dealt by essence." It is brought about by engaging life fully with all one's skill and courage in order to draw forth the great secrets of God hidden in the potentiality of one's human form— like a Michelangelo teasing the Pietà from the *bloc résistant.*

In terms of Boehme's earlier metaphor of the soul at the instant of its death glowing like a piece of iron, mobility would be the intensity of the incandescence—the brilliance with which the light of Christ presses through it. But majesty would be the beauty of the artifice: Is this piece of iron an intricately wrought grille, or simply an unarticulated lump? Majesty has to do with the power of actualization: the conscious shaping of the vessel that bears the light of Christ.

Dying to self...awakening to self: the two paths exist in creative tension within us. If mobility is won through the intensity of spiritual striving, majesty has more to do with the bringing forth of what is hidden within us and the integration of competing elements within us. It involves the yielding and giving aspects of our journey, whereas the former involves the pushing and driving. Between these contrary tensions—and in fact because of them—we make our way along, like a sailboat poised between the force of the wind on its sails and the tug of the water against its keel. The knack of finding one's innate sense of balance here is what I believe Helen Luke is referring to in her observation about wholeness emerging out of the acceptance of the conflict between the contrary strivings within us.

One fact that contemporary psychology has made eminently clear to us is that wholeness can come about only if we embrace the whole of ourselves—not only what is highest in us, but the shadow as well. For majesty to grow in us, all must come to the light, both the dark parts of oneself that need healing and the light parts that need birthing; and only the whole ball of wax, integrated and accepted, becomes "the wonders thou hast wrought and found out here." This is because majesty is the divine face of human wholeness. It is essence—who we really are—actualized and transposed to its full spiritual expression.

In the Kingdom of Heaven, majesty becomes the luminosity—the degree of magnification, or brilliance of expressivity—with which God's love is reflected in the soul. It is at the same time the measure of the soul's receptivity, the depth of its capacity to be filled with (hence, *bear*) divine love. And as on earth, so in heaven:

when it comes to luminosity, orders of magnitude vary greatly, with some souls clearly outshining others. As Boehme expresses it, "They shall excel one another as the stars of heaven; but there will be no grudging, but everyone will rejoice at the excellence of the other, for there is no other light than God, filling all in all."[1]

Normally, majesty must be attained in time—in bodily life—for majesty is precisely the measure of actualized essence, the path actually traveled. This is what I was driving at in my earlier comment that at the moment of death, when the template of our soul is illuminated by the light of Christ, "those parts that belong authentically to oneself but have not been fully actualized and integrated in life simply remain dark." And, of course, this would then be precisely the arena in which the notion of growth beyond death would take on a concrete and objective meaning: it would be the nurturing into the light of those authentic parts of our essence that in life had remained unarticulated or unfulfilled, so that we could unfold up to the full degree of our intended luminosity in the Kingdom of Heaven. I think this also fairly closely approximates what Gurdjieff was getting at in his notion of Holy Planet Purgatory—not a place of punishment, but of further development of one's innate potential and amplitude—"up to the highest degree of objective reason."

But how could that growth continue to take place once death has put an end to time? Faced with this logical impossibility, the West by and large looks to final judgment while the East looks to reincarnation, but there is still one more possibility. Love is stronger than death and can find ways of working beyond time and body—if the union of hearts is sufficiently deep.

WRESTLING

Let's return to the concrete: Rafe and me. I included the difficult story of our wrestling match because for me it contains the core

experience of how love actually works to set essence free. Its transforming power lies in the shadow work.

"Perhaps all the dragons in our lives are princesses who are only
waiting to see us act, just once, with beauty and courage," writes
Rilke in his *Letters to a Young Poet*.[2] In a single vivid metaphor he
encapsulates what I believe is the basic metaphysical principle by
which majesty is created in this life and grown in the next. The
most mysterious aspect of the kind of intimacy between two
beloveds on the path is the trust and intuitive support to wade into
and transform the worst in each other: those dragons deeply buried,
waiting to see us act, just once, with beauty and courage.

Before meeting Rafe, I had been married for nearly ten years to
a man with whom I was functionally soul-blind. We struggled
valiantly to make the relationship work, but the underlying malaise
always resurfaced. At the deepest level we didn't understand and
were afraid of—repelled by—each other's shadow side. He said
that I seemed alien and bizarre; I feared what appeared to be a
miasmal darkness and heaviness in his soul. In each of us was a barrier that the other could not cross, and the more the friction of
intimacy rubbed the wounds raw, the more firmly the defense
mechanisms were set in position to protect that dark, sleeping, and
yet vaguely sensed as precious place.

Such relationships are not only useless but dangerous. They are
a caricature of intimacy. For the deepest side of intimacy is that we
are invited inside the other; as love follows its natural path toward
what Bruteau calls the deepest, or "I-I" relationship—"to feel the
other on the inside, as the other feels"[3]—we stand in the midst of
one another's dragons, which must be regarded with infinite tenderness and compassion. To look upon them with loathing is a kind
of inner murder, like the fox minding the henhouse. Where such

murder is quietly taking place under the guise of relationship, the partners gradually become outer shells, trapped more and more in their personalities and increasingly numb on the inside. The dragons recede deeper and deeper into the unconscious.

That's who I was well on my way to becoming when I met Rafe. It didn't take long for things to start to turn around. What was striking from the start was an extraordinary emotional trust between us. Even early on, the innate grasp of who the other was allowed us to fall through the surface roles and postures and address each other from dead center. Rafe noticed it, too, and was markedly vitalized by it. But inevitably, what soon began to happen was that our sense of relief, safe haven in the other, brought us both to that inner boundary line that neither of us had ever crossed.

From the start, it seemed, we were on a converging course with that wrestling match in the dooryard that morning. All our little fights headed toward it, exposing the core issues while yet giving us the confidence of emerging each time stronger and more together. At last we were down to the primal terrors: Rafe feared and loathed emotional confinement; I was desperately afraid of abandonment, but paralyzed to express my fear and rage. The moment was finally at hand.

I still don't know exactly what triggered that moment. But we slammed into our worst terrors and were both shattered—and refashioned a huge step closer to who we really were. Even in the midst of the debacle, there was still a wild exaltation about it. I could feel my heart finally climbing free. It was my unabashed rage against losing Rafe that snapped me out of my long slumber of grief; plus somehow the trust that in an oblique way he would understand, as he did. He later told me that his *awe* that I could shatter so completely and still come through it whole gave him permission to open boxes within himself that had remained tightly padlocked and give free rein to that vulnerable and nurturing side in which his creative gifts could at last blossom.

What this means, of course, is that soulwork with an authentic soul partner can be messy, untidy, frequently turbulent. The beloved holds a key possessed by no one else, which allows him or her to plunge deeper into the other's psychic realms than any other human being, to unlock dungeons that even the beloved cannot open alone. This aspect of relationship was probably the most shocking to Rafe—to me as well—and for a while everything in his monastic training recoiled against it. Only after that fight, I think, did he come to see this as a gift and accept it into his life. But with that acceptance came a softening in him, a setting down of burdens long shouldered alone and a willingness to share much more freely his fears, childhood memories, and intimations of his approaching death. Those darkening weeks of late fall were in so many ways a springtime for both of us.

Earlier on, I observed that in the struggle for wholeness with Rafe, it was our worst features and not our best that were transformed to make the new person. I believe this observation is not only personally accurate, but reflects a more general metaphysical formula, which goes as follows:

> "dragon"   +   unconditional love   =   "princess"
> (hidden essence...   transformed in love...   yields Real I)

What this formula means is that essence—who we really are, the heart of our hearts—seems truly and mysteriously to be bound up with our hiddenness and pain. Underneath those wounds, closely guarded in the place where we most instinctively draw back and hide, lies our most innate and vulnerable sense of selfhood, our seed of the Holy Particularity, the Name of God we bear. It is hidden precisely because it is the treasure in the field, the pearl of great price.

But who will unlock it? Healing in the modern sense—the bringing to consciousness and release of the pain—in some ways mistakes the corn for the husk, in the sense that we think that by getting rid of the pain we will be free to be who we really are. But the real process is more subtle. In fact, who we really are is the person revealed walking, like Shadrach in the fiery furnace, in the center of that moment when the pain meets and is illuminated by unconditional love. It is a new creation. That instant itself is the dawn of Real I, the breakthrough of the majesty into the human realm. And to live and share this with a human partner is to experience what Mouravieff calls the "baptism of fire,"[4] the work of intense fusion that more and more allows that Real I to become the permanently experienced seat of individuality.

CHAPTER 15

THE ABLER SOUL

IT WASN'T EXACTLY A HOLLYWOOD first meeting. Neither one of us felt a tingling in every fiber of our being at having found the other half of our soul. But in its own way, that first conversation between Rafe and me that snowy December morning in the monastery barnyard was quietly extraordinary. As our words poured forth into the sparkling sunlight, perhaps the most remarkable aspect of our encounter was the sense of spaciousness and ancient ease with each other, as if somehow we had never been strangers. A few months later, trying to express this mysterious sense of completeness between us, Rafe said, "I don't know who I am, but I feel *right*—like a boat that's not listing."

Like most of Rafe's one-liners, it hit the nail on the head. A boat will straighten up in the water when the ballast has been shifted to true center, and that was essentially the experience for both of us in relationship. There was a sense of coming to an inner balance that had so long eluded us separately because all along it had lain in the whole. Like two puzzle pieces interlocking to reveal the larger picture, we began to discover, particularly in those blessed last weeks of our human walk together, how in each other the confused and broken gestures of a lifetime finally made sense.

In the weeks immediately following Rafe's death, by far the most anguished part of my grief was the fear that this magical process between us would now come to an end. To have seen the puzzle coming together only to have it ripped apart again seemed cruel beyond measure. It was not so much *my* wholeness I mourned, but *our* wholeness: the chance to emerge fully into those unknown but amazing people we were starting to become in the light of each other's love. Only gradually have I begun to understand the truth of what Rafe was trying to teach me that night when he pointed so sharply to the full moon behind the crescent and said, "That's us!" When the wholeness is there—seen or unseen—the sliver need have no fear about how it will grow.

Now, three years beyond Rafe's death, I am beginning to be more comfortable in owning that Rafe and I belonged to—and still belong to—that class of relationships known as "abler souls." I borrow the term from John Donne (although the category itself is of far greater antiquity, first recorded in Western literature by Plato) to describe a relationship marked by a peculiarly intense conviction of belonging to a whole that is greater than the sum of its parts.[1] Far more than a partnership, it is a kinship that is intuitively recognized.

The abler soul is a reasonably rare configuration even among committed love partnerships, which may be why it is so persistently overlooked in the Christian teachings on the soul after death. The closest approximation would be an eternal marriage, but even this term, with its usual fuzzy overtones of "true love," obscures more than it reveals. The abler soul *is* a path of true love, but not in the way we commonly think of it—intensely, passionately romantic—

but rather true in the sense that it conforms to and reveals the authentic pattern of each partner's soul—and this is the key to the whole idea. During life, the innate sense of wholeness between the partners makes for an unusual ease and comfort in their relationship. And after death, if the groundwork has been adequately laid, it offers the one clear window of opportunity acknowledged in our tradition (however obliquely) for continued mutual soulwork.

I am convinced that it is the category of abler souls that Jacob Boehme has in mind when he makes his one cryptic exception to the rule "After death, there is no bettering, but everything remains the way it is." Under certain conditions—when the experienced sense of kinship and complementarity between partners runs so deep that the intimation begins to arise in them that their two individualities are really part of one whole, and when second body has developed to a point that it is possible for them to share in each other's "book of life" beyond the physical body—then they can by means of a conscious vow (or "earnest promise," in Boehme's words) dissolve the boundaries of their individual, smaller selves— "lay down their souls," in the biblical language of this teaching— and cast their lot entirely with that one abler soul they already sense themselves to be. At the death of one, that abler soul becomes a sheltering principle around *both* of them that will allow them to continue their common journey, exchanging the very marrow of their lives and actualizing and strengthening that one Real I between them. The final harvest of their soul's majesty will come at the death of the surviving partner.

If this sounds like special privilege, it is not. The tradition teaches that the abler soul is always given from above, not created from below; it seems to have a peculiar affinity with death and nearly always has something to do with cosmic servanthood. To accept the invitation to forge an abler soul is a virtually certain bet that one will be "nailed on earth." For true love is given to mirror and manifest God on earth, and not for self-realization and personal happiness. With the acceptance of those terms, the path comes into being.

PRECONDITIONS

One of the reasons I prefer Donne's term *abler soul* to the more common *soul mates* or *polar beings* is that it implicitly reminds us that the abler soul must be forged. An abler soul does not appear automatically, even in those relationships marked by an unusual passion and intimacy, but must "flow" (in Donne's words) from the two souls' conscious decision to become One. Nor can it be formed from the level of personality, no matter how sincere the intentions of the partners or compatible their interests; it always bears witness to a deep essence connection. A natural proclivity must undergird conscious choice, and in general those capable of forming abler souls will be drawn from a fairly narrow band. They will be beloveds in whose relationship the following three conditions are present:

1. A strong erotic connection between the partners.
2. An equally strong spiritual yearning and a maturity of spiritual experience independently acquired.
3. An innate emotional trust that enables their shadow work to unfold at the deepest levels of self-exposure and intimacy.

Even the presence of these three conditions does not guarantee that the partners will be able to consummate an abler soul between them, but it suggests strongly that the potential is there and offers rich ground for soulwork if the partners are sufficiently motivated. With this in mind, let me say a bit more about each of them.

"*A Strong Erotic Connection*"

The reason this is so—and why abler souls must always be beloveds and not some other type of essence connection (such as parent and child, siblings, friends)—is that the erotic, or sexual, energy is the specific energy through which this union of souls comes about. Sexual energy provides the force of fusion that holds the two formerly separate individualities in the nuclear bonding of one soul.

This is the teaching I believe J. G. Bennett was specifically referring to in that passage Rafe was so taken with: "For certain very high purposes it is essential that man acquire a soul [an abler soul, or a true and actualized experience of one's own Real I]. The normal way of doing this is through the union of the sexes."

Union of the sexes does not necessarily mean physical intercourse, as Bennett himself specifically points out a few sentences later. In the inner tradition (from which these teachings mostly emerge), sexual energy is understood as something very different from libido, or lust, which is how the term is almost inevitably interpreted in contemporary culture. It is the highest form of transformational energy, the finest and most subtle spiritual energy that human beings can work with directly while still in a physical body. Sexual energy is the agent of all transformation—not just physical procreation, but every form of creativity: prayer, poetry, and spiritual transformation. It does not necessarily imply genital sexuality, although it does not preclude it either. But in either case, the union of sexes that Bennett refers to is at a far more subtle level than physical intercourse and may well be hindered rather than aided by an expression at this coarser level.

While erotic energy does not necessarily imply genital sexuality, it does imply a deep equality between the two partners, a flow-

ing out to one another in a complete mutuality of personhood.
Vladimir Solovyov, the great nineteenth-century Russian philosopher of love, is the only one I know to have seen so clearly the enormous implication of this point, which defines both the process of
the erotic love and its ultimate destination:

> The meaning and worth of love…is that it really forces us,
> with all our being, to acknowledge for *another* the same
> absolute central significance which, because of the power of
> our egoism, we are conscious of only in our own selves. Love
> is important not as one of our feelings, but…as the shifting
> of the very center of our personal lives. This is characteristic
> of every kind of love, but predominantly of sexual love [erotic
> love]; it is distinguished from other kinds of love by greater
> intensity, by a more engrossing character, and by the possibil-
> ity of more complete overall reciprocity. Only this love can
> lead to the real and indissoluble union of two lives into one;
> only of it do the words of Holy Writ say: "They shall be one
> flesh," that is, shall become one real being.[2]

This deep sense of give-and-take (or "complete overall reciprocity," in Solovyov's words) is what distinguishes the soulwork of
beloveds beyond the grave from the more classic guru/disciple
transmission, which also involves an exchange of spiritual energy,
or *baraka*, across the grave, but flowing from the higher to the
lower—from the one who is complete to the one who is not. It is
the continuing mutuality of our encounters (and hence, the elements of freshness and surprise) that ultimately dissuades me from
seeing my relationship with Rafe as a transmission story. Those
aspects are there, of course, but the essential flavor of our journey is
that continued headlong plunge into pure becoming in which the
outcome remains open-ended for both of us. There is something

more static about the guru/disciple transmission; the erotic path is pure dynamism.

"*Spiritual Yearning and Maturity*"

Boris Mouravieff provides the core text for this teaching in his classic study of spiritual love in *Gnosis*. Affirming that the fusion of two beloveds into one Real I is indeed a true path to salvation, he nonetheless cautions: "In practice, this can only happen when the two personalities are very advanced, and both rich with the experience each has separately acquired in exterior life."[3]

The reasons for this caution are probably stated as well as by anyone in Rilke's inspired seventh "Letter to a Young Poet," where he warns lovers to hold their own against the overwhelming urge to meld into each other—"for what would a union be of two people who are unclarified, unfinished, and still incoherent?" Real love, he says, "is a high inducement for the individual to ripen, to become something in himself, to become world, to become world in himself for the sake of another person."[4] In modern terminology, such a premature merger out of desperate needs and fuzzy boundaries would be called codependency. By contrast, the abler soul is abler: its essential earmark, according to Mouravieff, is a "freedom in unity," which allows the partners to function well even when physically separated.

My own observation, however, is that the abler-soul configuration is intrinsically not codependent, and the difference in taste will be obvious, even when the partners are very young in chronological years. Mature life experience certainly refines the mechanisms of discernment and will in most cases have laid useful groundwork in "breaking through the crust of personality" (as Mouravieff terms it). But it is not a prerequisite for meeting one's soulmate or even a reliable indicator of success in building the partnership into a full spiritual union. I do not think Rafe and I could have met before we did; we would have been too self-involved to recognize each other. But my daughter Lucy and her husband, Alby, who met each other in their early twenties, from the very start displayed that "freedom in unity"[5] that in time, and with work, I have no doubt will emerge into a true spiritual union. In this sense, then, I believe "maturity of life experience" is better translated as "readiness as determined by God." The abler soul, recall, is given from above.

The other stipulation holds firm, however: there must be a strong spiritual yearning—at least if the partnership is to have hope of maturing into a union that will endure beyond the grave. That is because—as I intimated earlier and as is strongly stated in a single sentence by an anonymous contemporary master—"true love demands sacrifice because true love is a transforming force and is really the birth-pangs of union at a higher level."[6]

In a single, stark sentence this writer foreshadows both the sublime potential of this path and the suffering that may be entailed to arrive there. At the very least, the sacrifice required of the partners will be a laying down of their separate centers of gravity (the metaphor that both Solovyov and Rafe used) in the effort to form a conscious union of wills—far deeper and more binding than in ordinary marriage. At the ultimate, this laying down of self can extend to their very lives.

I mentioned earlier that true love seems to have a strong affinity with death. Perhaps it is more accurate to say it has a strong affinity with eternity. True love has no great regard for the boundary between life and death, which is invisible to it anyway; the only thing that matters is that relentless drive toward complete self-giving. Like the candle flame, it will come alive only by expending itself utterly. This is the Shiva-like aspect of true love, creating-and-destroying, that must be accepted as a given along with the gift.

There must be a strong spiritual yearning—strong enough to withstand the loneliness and ache of the flesh of this world—because whether it lasts a lifetime or only a brief space of months or weeks, the arena where this love will truly come into its own is "at the intersection of the timeless with time," in T. S. Eliot's words. And the exchanges will be within terms of the substances proper to the body of hope: conscious love, courage, plenitude, faith. What the two partners can do together in life to build up these reserves will be crucial when those "birth-pangs of a union at a higher level" set in in earnest. In its strictest sense, the tradition teaches that unless their human work together has brought them to the critical level of spiritual maturation known as "permanent individuality," no further development is possible beyond the grave, no matter how ardent their love. While I am personally unwilling to place such severe restrictions on the free-flowing creativity of love, it is fair to reiterate what I said earlier: the more second body is developed within them, the more the two partners will become fluent and expressive in "next year's language."

"A Deep, Intuitive Emotional Trust"

More than anything else, I believe the shadow work between the partners is the real holy ground in their relationship: untidy, messy, alchemical, holy. For what is brought into being, through it, this abler soul or joint Real I, is not simply a blending together but a fusion at a higher level. It is a new creation (as Bennett rightly observes), forged chiefly through the melting down of each one's chains in the fires of unconditional love. Charles Upton speaks to this point when he writes: "In genuine romantic love the fire of emotional and sexual passion is alchemical not concupiscent: burning away the dross of egotism and synthesizing the Philosopher's Stone...the power of divine grace working in human relations."[7] The abler soul is a function of purification, not passion. It comes to pass only in the refiner's fire of the unconditional giving of self, which is the unique and sacred thing that abler souls intuitively know how to do for one another.

From my own observations, I believe that the quality of their shadow work is the most reliable indicator of whether an abler soul may be in the works for two partners. It is not how they relate during their better times, what inspired quests or common visions they share, but rather, how they work together to unlock and heal each other's dragons. The techniques can be learned, but the knack is essentially God-given.

THE FIFTH WAY

In the Christian inner tradition, this path of the intense fusion of two beloveds into one abler soul has sometimes been called "the Fifth Way." The term itself is of fairly recent vintage, coined by Boris Mouravieff in imitation of Gurdjieff's Fourth Way, although the teaching it conveys is ancient. If the Fourth Way is the way of consciousness, the Fifth Way is the way of radical meltdown through total self-abandonment in love. There is a beloved objectively other than oneself, and the distinguishing feature of this path is that the true self resides not in the "I," but in the "we"—in the abler soul that emerges in the union.

The path is elusive because it so easily mutates into something else: at one end of the spectrum, romantic tragedy—Romeo and Juliet, Tristan and Isolde, the whole gamut of star-crossed lovers; at the other end, celibate monastic love, where the beloved is identified as Christ. To hold its fine edge as a spiritual path that commits itself to spiritual transformation through the passionate love for a particular human person is a difficult balancing act, but at least in its essential form, that's what the Fifth Way is. The core of the teaching is about how two *human* beloveds come together to fuse their one permanent abler soul, which contains their unique and imperishable identity, or Real I. Monastic love mysticism—the form in which this tradition is predominantly handed on today—represents an elaborate allegorization of this originally flesh-and-blood reality.[8]

In the terms I have been using in this book, attaining Real I—also known in the tradition as "permanent individuality"—means that in such a person mobility and majesty are developed to the point that he or she moves in the Kingdom of Heaven as a real presence, an amplitude. Such a person will not merely rest, in the classic theological sense, but can continue to be active and expressive in the service of God and, under certain circumstances, to grow. This seemingly minor point is actually of major significance.

The Fifth Way has sometimes been seen as a spiritual shortcut for exactly this reason: the couple's Real I resides in their joint abler soul. Working together, the partners receive several enormous boosts: the confidence that comes from sensing their common whole; the boldness with which they can plow through their shadow work; and above all, the willingness to die to self, which is the real crucible of transformation. The very intensity of the desire they have to give all to the other will become the bridge on which they cross from passion to *com*passion.[9]

POLAR BEINGS?

But do they originally have to have been one being? That is the ancient and most mythological version of the theory of the bipolar soul, which has captivated mystical imagination from Plato right down through Mouravieff.[10] If this stipulation holds true—that the partners are a singular, eternally foreordained match and that none but this unique partner will produce the desired spiritual results—then, regrettably, the Fifth Way path is open only to those who have already miraculously located their needle-in-a-haystack soul mate. It is this highly romanticized version of the teaching, I believe, that has contributed so heavily to the general distrust of true love as a spiritual path. The quest for authentic transformation is sentimentalized into a quest for the perfect partner, and as one waits on the bank for one's knight in shining armor or *dame de ses pensées* to appear, it is all too easy to daydream one's life away.

I now see that the solution to this koan is really simple. The problem lies in our limited and time-bound notion of the word *original.* Judged from the standpoint of earth, *original* means "first in time." From the standpoint of heaven it means "whole in purpose"—and quite unlike linear time, divine life flows out in concentric circles from that center of wholeness. When our destiny moves into right alignment with God, what is inevitable in our path will come to be; "first" or "afterwards" does not matter. If we are intended to walk a Fifth Way path, the partner we are to walk it with will inevitably appear. Meanwhile, if the way keeps opening, keep on walking.

I do not have a clue whether Rafe and I were originally a bipolar soul. Neither of us ever resonated with the sense of being the other's only and eternal soul mate (at least not that we would admit to), and both of us had known romances more impassioned and consuming. What I do know is that from early on we both somehow understood that we were entrusted to each other for the next leg of the journey, and neither of us, however tough the going got, ever seriously thought of quitting. The way kept opening, and we kept walking—through sadness and laughter and healing, through locked dungeons in each other's soul that no person had ever opened before...into death and through it and beyond. That is all I know, and probably all I need to know. The way keeps opening and we still keep on walking.

THE VOW

BUT TO RETURN TO THE HEART of the matter: Boehme specifies quite clearly that in order for the abler soul potentiality to emerge into a fully fledged spiritual union that will "comprehend" the two beloveds in their soulwork beyond the grave, there must be an "earnest promise" sworn. The word Boehme uses for "promised," *verloben,* implies even more narrowly that this "earnest promise" is specifically a love vow, a betrothal, and that it must be sworn "in the time of this life." Did Rafe and I do that?

I believe we did—though just barely. And with this in mind, I want to return now to Rafe's funeral wake and reconstruct what I believe was going on between us in that luminous night.

I know that what I am about to share may seem crazy. For three years I have not really dared to let myself believe it, but it keeps coming back to me as the simplest and truest explanation and the only one that accounts for all the puzzle pieces. It explains the distinctly nuptial feeling-tone of the night and why my experience of Rafe as a present and intimate partner has intensified over time rather than diminished. It also accounts for that peculiar, persistent sense that we are living one life, and that this life is not simply a re-creation of his life as he taught it to me, but somehow a whole new ball game for both of us. The story may sound crazy, but the pieces fit. So here goes my version.

Rafe, I am convinced, was destined for mastery—one whose soaring life of prayer is carried easily within himself, in the full integration of his human personhood. Such a man is a bodhisattva in the East, one charged with a unique mission of maintaining and nurturing the spiritual life of the planet. He belongs to the "conscious circle of humanity"—the term Rafe himself was most comfortable with and to which he aspired ardently.

Now there are two ways of fulfilling this role as a higher cosmic servant. One is through the most extreme forms of solitary devotion—the hermit cliff-dwellers of India or the Syrian desert, for example, whose whole life is spent "yielded between" heaven and earth (in Helen Luke's words) in powerful intercessory prayer. The other is through the exercise of conscious mastery in the human plane: as a teacher, a master and guide, a creative genius. These complementary types are classically illustrated in the craggy and mysterious Shams, who touched down on earth only long enough to pass on his divine knowledge to another human being; and his beloved disciple Rumi, who stayed behind to illumine the hearts of so many through his ecstatic outpouring of poetry and dance.

While Rafe always saw himself as belonging to the former category, there were clear signs that he was actually cut far more from the second bolt. There was a natural fineness to his being, no matter how hard he tried to cover it up, and an innately cultured and philosophical turn of mind that, if developed, would have lent amazing scope to the fierceness of his spiritual striving. Not many knew, looking at the rough-hewn little guy who shuffled around in his greasy work jeans fixing old snowmobiles, that there was another side to his heritage as well. The French aristocrat was strong in his blood. His family line had directly descended from a surgeon and general in Napoleon's army who established himself in Louisiana after the Napoleonic wars, and Rafe's own branch of the family traces itself through six generations of wealthy and well-respected planters in the bayou country of St. Landry Parish. His great-uncle was midway through his term as governor of Louisiana the year that Rafe was born.

But the other side was true as well. For equally running through that family blood were the demons of alcoholism and depression. Nearly twenty years younger than his brother and sisters, Rafe—then Louis Numa Robin Jr.—spent a lonely and somewhat unsettled childhood, with frequent moves around the state following the boom-and-bust cycles of his father's livestock-trading business. The uncertain circumstances of his upbringing, and then a family tragedy that shattered his life when he was fifteen, left him wary and adrift. For the next fifteen years he ran wild, hurtling through the navy, a long stint in the merchant marine, commercial flight school, drunken fights, broken romances, and finally a profound religious conversion on his brother's dairy farm in Mississippi.

"How do you *know* there's a God?" the cocky young pilot taunted his brother, Sam.

"Just look around you," said Sam.

Rafe looked around him—and he never stopped looking.

But even then the old demons remained, making those first tender years of his journey toward God a constant battle of three steps forward and two steps back. At last, terrified of his sexuality, his outbursts of rage, and the alcoholism that ran so strongly in his family, Rafe took himself out of the running—out of the world and into the confinement of a monastery and eventually a hermitage—in order to work on himself before God in the only way he knew how.

It was an act of great spiritual courage. I have never met a man with more courage than Rafe, a man who could get so far on so little, using only the naked intensity of his yearning for God to propel him along the path. And in time, this bore fruit within him, and the supersensual gifts of prayer began to grow. By the time I met him, he had become something of a local legend—at least to those who could see beneath the surface. His long years of working on himself had paid off; he had become a conscious man, balanced and largely in control of himself.

A "pneumatikos" of the old school, formed in the classic desert tradition of spiritual warfare, Rafe had his mobility in spades. But as is so often the case with veterans of this path, his mobility had been bought at the expense of his majesty, that vast and remarkable essence in him that also begged for expression. Those long years of solitary self-renunciation were also a deliberate choice to leave many gifts in himself untapped.

Like so many of his forebears in the mystical life—including his slightly older contemporary Thomas Merton—Rafe had a pronounced penchant for equating true self with pure interiority. All the "characteristics," as he called them—those distinct, particular features of his essence—belonged to the old man, the one that was falling away, and only by the sheer mortification of his human nature could the new man come to be.

I remember a conversation I once had with him in one of those times of unusual clarity between us. "So, Rafe," I asked him directly, "what *is* your aim?"

"Let me preface this," he began quite formally after a moment or so of reflection, "by saying there is a me with certain character-istics."

"Frenchman? Temper?" I asked.

"Yes. And as that—the old man—diminishes, something else is able to be present. And so my aim is to hew the line deeper. To go farther and farther into God...to disappear into God."

This deep bent toward the renunciation of your human essence in order to "disappear into God" is a pervasive tendency of the Christian apophatic life, of which Rafe was a true son. To the extent that it favors the divine striving over the human integration, it is a distortion—at least if Helen Luke's road map of wholeness is correct. But it is a magnificent distortion, creating in its most deter-mined seekers a fierce, wild rake to the soul, like the spruce trees on a wintry coast bent to the prevailing wind. At whatever the indi-vidual cost, the trees point to the stark reality of the wind and in the very solemnity of their pointing take on some of its numinous power. That was the man I saw standing before me in the barnyard that blazing December morning, a circle of light almost palpably enfolding him as he took both my hands and gazed intently into my eyes: proud, defiant, holy, shy, lost—all of the above.

What met Rafe's own gaze that day in the barnyard was in some ways the perfect mirror. Standing before him in my old ski knickers and baseball cap, I looked to him, as he later confessed, about twenty years old. Like Rafe, life had bent me far downstream of my real compass track. Frightened and rebellious, I hid my womanhood beneath a tomboy exterior and ran from my Ph.D. and mile-long string of admissions cards to the credentialed world to hide out in an island fishing village and then among the monks and ranchers of this mountain valley. On the surface I was wiry and supremely self-reliant; underneath was a tentative and vulnerable

woman whose languishing gifts as an artist and teacher were somehow bound up in her deeply buried femininity. That was the one
Rafe saw standing before him that day as our eyes searched for the
meaning of this strange, providential encounter. Even then I think
both of us sensed vaguely that we were about to call the question
on each other.

THE WEAVING

And thus, between us began a kind of secret fugue. If its subject
was our spiritual high striving and the passing on of the hermit's
path, the countersubject was the almost delicious secret glee we
took in recognizing who the other was—the secret artist and aristocrat at the helm. At the Stanley, we made cappuccino and bouil-
labaisse. He was fascinated by my music and books. Sometimes we
spoke French. And he told me tales of his planter ancestors and his
childhood in the bayous, and he spent the last of a small inheri-
tance from his sister to buy me a beautiful silk suit. We read *The
Brothers Karamazov* together and cooked jambalaya and raised our
mugs to "the deepening celebration." And each of us could feel
something coming alive in us that had so long slept.

And there was the day when he told me, in a moment of heart-
felt sincerity, "I want to integrate my past, all of who I am, and give
it to you."

But right there was the problem. For how can you integrate
something you are also simultaneously trying to renounce? As long
as the fugue remained in secret, the right hand not knowing what
the left was doing, all was well between us, but whenever we tried
to confront the two opposing scenarios directly, we always came up
against the same anguishing stuck point. The old patterning would
lift for a while, but then like the fog it would drop down again, that

old formation that said so strongly true self can only be pure interiority...pure interiority. Seeing those fresh new blossoms budding
on both our branches was wondrous to Rafe, but it was also deeply
disorienting, and he could finally react only with ambivalence and
dismay. His lifelong pursuit of pure becoming compelled him to
cast away all way stations, even those of his own emerging wholeness. He sensed the abler soul growing between us—we both did—
but he was terrified of it.

During those last weeks together we were bearing down on
that final barrier. But still he hung back, afraid of betraying his
post, fearing and distrustful of his characteristics. To the end he
insisted that "I love you" is not something human beings can truth-
fully say; he feared that his growing human love was a "hindrance"
(as he called it) to his divine striving. He died with that tension still
unresolved between us.

At the moment of his death I believe it resolved.

"A Gambler's Heart"

In those extraordinary next three days, Rafe did not fully depart
from his body. He hovered close, knowing how desperately I
yearned for that final encounter in the human flesh and how ready
he himself was to give it. I don't know what usually happens at the
moment of death, but I have a strong sense that Rafe held back,
declined an immediate immersion in beatific grace, out of concern
for me and the unresolved business between us. He took the risk
that I would be able to recognize and respond to the strong signal
of his will, that I would find my way to his side, and through the
mask of death. When we finally came together that night in the
chapel, our hearts and souls melted into each other, and in that
complete self-giving in love, we entered and passed through the

baptism of fire, that supreme alchemy of the Fifth Way path, into the eternal union of our souls.

Sometime during the wee hours of that night, kneeling by his side, I slipped my right hand into his. When I released it, I noticed that the silver ring he'd given me for my birthday the year before was shining a soft, luminous gold. I slipped the ring onto my left finger, where it has stayed to this day. I thought the golden glow was a reflection of the light in the chapel, but it remained even after I left at dawn, and all through the funeral mass later that morning. Only after Rafe's body had been laid in the grave did it gradually fade.

And so the earnest promise was sealed between us, and in that night, I believe, we both dissolved and were born again as our joint Real I, the abler soul between us. There is no "me" anymore and no "Rafe"—only the open vein of our love, holding us both true to the new path of becoming. The individual poles remain, but the unit of wholeness is the "us." And the final harvest of the majesty is now in both our hands.

Perhaps you might call it a gamble: that the two of us, working together, can become far more than either one of us could alone. But in my heart, I feel the matter much more simply: that Rafe did what he did simply because he loved me. And because he saw this was my best chance—perhaps my only chance—to fulfill my own destiny. Really, there is no gamble in love because it is all death, all laying down.

Several months after Rafe's death, in the midst of wrestling over a new job possibility in British Columbia, I was frightened out of sleep by a nightmare that graphically revealed my deepest fears. To get to the place where Rafe and I would be reunited—so the dream went—I had boarded a bus full of people, only to discover after an hour headed in the wrong direction that no driver was on board! Time was running out; I knew the only way to get to my destination was to drive the bus myself, and I knew I had the skills to do it. But I was afraid. I made a few awkward attempts to win permission from the other passengers, but they ignored me, and I lost heart. I got off the bus and was left stranded. It was my life-long fear of failure again, right there in my face.

Terrified, I fled up to the cabin and was sitting in the old chair, sobbing, when Rafe's voice came, gentle but firm:

"Open your eyes. Look at me."

I did. Not that I could see him, I knew, but maybe he could see me—blue eyes gazing back at him in trust and love. I did, and yes, for the first time, directly in front of me, I saw light—not bright and fiery like St. Paul's fireball, but golden and infinitely gentle, like that night in the monastery chapel. Then ever so softly the speaking continued: "Don't be afraid. I laid down my life so that my strength would be in you."

That was all he said. It was enough.

During his life Rafe had a word to describe the quality of our relationship: he called it our "concern" for each other, and he promised that no matter what happened between us, I would always have it. At the time I resisted the word, thinking that it described some vague, generic affection based on worry or duty. Only in the light of his death was I finally able to see that what he had been talking about all along was simply the spontaneous self-giving that comes from a sheer delight in each other's being, and from the wish at the center of one's heart that the other be well. Free from the self-righteousness of duty, or even the compulsion of romantic attraction, it simply "leans and harkens" after the other, in John Donne's words, never forgetting, never failing to consider the other's good—even from beyond the grave. Some would call it conscious love. It is the pearl of great price I had been seeking all my life, but always in the wrong place. Because I couldn't command it, I thought it wasn't love. Only through Rafe did I finally come to realize that's exactly why it is.

CHAPTER 17

LOVE AND DEATH

"LOVE AND DEATH HAVE A COMMON ROOT," says Ladis-laus Boros. "The best love-stories end in death, and this is no accident. Love is, of course, and remains the triumph over death, but that is not because it abolishes death but because it is itself death. Only in death is the total surrender that is love's possible, for only in death can we be exposed completely and without reserve. That is why lovers go so simply and unconcernedly to their death, for they are not entering a strange country; they are going into the inner chamber of love."[1]

Strange, unsettling words.... And yet I cannot say they are not true. While it is certainly possible that a couple on a genuine Fifth Way path might live to a ripe old age together, the whole aspect of brevity seems to be built in, like those little wildflowers Rafe and I spoke of that work faster at the higher altitudes. Love and death are inextricably linked, because it is the very office of this kind of love to demonstrate that love *is* stronger than death, to melt the mask of death in the waters of pure self-giving.

In retrospect, I can name quite clearly the moment when Rafe and I crossed the point of no return. We both knew at the time that something was happening, but we didn't know what.

It came one particular week toward the end of May 1995, as my time at the Stanley place drew to a close. I had not been able to turn up a single affordable rental in the area, and meanwhile an interesting job prospect was shaping up in British Columbia. It looked like the handwriting was on the wall for Rafe's and my time together.

We worked hard all that week to adjust ourselves to the new reality. After a last moving farewell over a cup of cappuccino, we tried to help each other withdraw emotionally, resume those old teacher/student roles long left behind. He said it was time for the little bird to fly out of the nest. I thanked him for all he had taught me and promised to stay in touch. He said he would pray for me. We both looked down at the floor a lot. And perhaps at that point we could still, just barely, have pulled apart—I on to new adventures, always carrying a piece of him in my heart; Rafe back to the cabin to process and integrate the rich new pieces of himself that our time together had yielded.

But it didn't work out that way. Down to the wire before leaving for British Columbia, I spent a final night in solitude at his cabin. There in the wee hours of the darkness I awoke in the middle of a vivid, captivating dream that my old childhood home was burning down, the old brick-and-gingerbread Victorian that my mother had named the Valentine House. But strangely enough, it was a slow fire, green and gold—not red and angry—and its progress was also somehow a new beginning, like the green buds just emerging on the hillsides above the monastery.

I didn't know exactly what I'd seen and heard in this excruciatingly Jungian dream, but moment by moment its import grew more certain. "No!" I wrote in my journal as first light gathered in the sky, "I do not in my heart of hearts believe that Rafe's and my earthly time has run its course." I walked down from the cabin, bumped into a ranching neighbor with a spare bedroom to rent, and within an hour had a place to stay.

Rafe was waiting for me back at the Stanley place when I got there. I don't know exactly what went on for him that night—he never directly said—but the green and gold fire was burning in his eyes. We fell into each other's arms and hugged for a long, long time. When we finally found words again, the first ones he spoke were, "I tried to protect myself by giving it a shape, but it has no shape. All I can do is open my heart more and more deeply."

Did we know we were both opening our hearts to death? Yes and no. Would it have made any difference? I have replayed that moment over and over in my mind and still could not choose otherwise. "At least we both want the same thing," Rafe had said during that conversation. And though I ache for what it cost, I realize we could not and would not have found what we did in those months remaining to us with any less willingness, with a scrap of self-preservation or common sense. "The total surrender that is love's" is what we both wanted, and we knew our hearts were set on it wherever it led.

It was in one sense completely pointless, like that wonderful O. Henry story "The Gift of the Magi," in which the two destitute lovers, to give each other a Christmas present, each surrender their most precious possession: she cuts and sells her beautiful long hair to buy him a chain for his gold watch; meanwhile he has sold his gold watch to buy her combs for her beautiful hair. So it is in true love: a pointless sacrifice. Unless the love itself is the point.

That love at this depth so often leads to death is a risk that must be accepted at the outset. I do not think this is because God punishes those who truly love, but because of the intensity of the fusion—and because, if Boros is right, death itself now appears in a new light, as the place where that "total surrender that is love's" can completely and unreservedly express itself. Once that surrender has been fully made, death has served its purpose and drops away to reveal the fullness of love.

WORKING IN

THE WONDERS

ABOUT A MONTH BEFORE HIS DEATH, Rafe came down off the hill one afternoon all excited about a passage he'd been pondering in a book by the theologian Paul Ricoeur. "A wager!" Rafe reported. "Ricoeur says that hermeneutics is always a wager— a wager that if your premise is right, you will live it into action."

For an old gambler like Rafe, that passage spoke worlds. But in the time since his death, it has also become a cornerstone of my own journey. If what I wager is true—that Rafe and I consciously bound our lives together that night in the chapel; that my visceral sense of a center still holding firm between us is in fact the abler soul at work; and that this larger and more purposeful soul is bending us both to a new course of becoming that neither of us could have chosen on our own—then I will discover if this is so in the attempt to live it out. And that is the road map for this second leg of the journey.

I have already written of Boehme's suggestion that this journey of love beyond the grave has something to do with "working in the wonders"—continuing to grow the soul by healing the dark parts and bringing to birth the untapped gifts. It is the same motion that

Rafe and I had already come to know so well; it is what love *does*—only now it does it in the body of hope. Here, in the sheltering matrix of that earnest promise jointly vowed, the true reciprocity that is love's can continue to unfold its wonders. And it is "the wonders thou hast wrought and found out here," Boehme reminds, that "maketh majesty in the soul."

With these as my basic orientation points, I am able to make some sense of the terrain now at hand, and to see this in-between time "not as a breach but an expansion," in John Donne's words—a time for the growth and deepening of love in wonderful and subtle ways, and hopefully with reverberations beyond just our own story. For if love is stronger than death—the hermeneutical premise that some few beloveds in every generation get elected to live into action in a particularly intense and sacramental way—then the crossing of this apparent desert is in some way also a sacred passage. Once you get used to it, it has its own unexpected beauty.

THE COMFORT OF PURPOSE

From the start it seemed that Rafe and I were headed for this passage. Ours was not a love in ordinary time and space. We were given a little human time to play in, and a miraculous sense of being called and held together as we lived out that first leg of the journey. The Stanley held, the water held, funds held, and despite the hesitations and backtrackings, *we* held. But that sense of imminent parting was also there, underlying everything we said or did. It is as if the gift of love deeper and more transforming than I would ever have believed possible in human flesh came with the built-in condition that the flesh would all too soon be left behind.

The simplest way of looking at our relationship, which people often suggest to me, is that I was sent into Rafe's life to help him complete what was necessary before he died. To a certain extent this is true: during our time together he broke through a lot of old conditioning and discovered an unknown side of himself in his gifts of nurturance and commitment. But I am not so sure this was completion, but more a foretaste of the majesty in him waiting to become fully expressive. During our time together we opened a lot more questions than we resolved, and if toward the end Rafe began to spread his wings, it was most likely because they were meant to fly!

If Rafe didn't die complete, as I suspect, but rather with the seed of continuance planted in him, one explanation may have to do with his full emergence into conscious mastery, into the conscious circle of humanity he so admired and aspired to. Because Rafe's vast spirit and enormous gifts were intended to come to fruition in a destiny of cosmic servanthood, the means were provided for the soulmaking to go on even after his body had ceased to be. That was the purpose for which I was led to Colorado, and the reason our love was appointed as the otherwise strangely incongruous final chapter to Rafe's life of solitary striving.

Working together in an abler soul means that you have to get used to thinking in terms of the whole organism, not the individual parts, and of pulling together toward a common good. If those glimpses of the Rafe I saw in the last weeks of his life—self-confident, creative, full of savoir faire—were any indication of things to come, then Rafe was clearly headed toward "the consolidation and integration of powers,"[1] and that is our highest common good.

And so what makes most sense in terms of the overall goal is not to repeat the part he has already done, but to stay right there on the breaking edge of what was becoming: emergence into wholeness through the reconciliation of pure interiority with the conscious exercise of our gifts. And the best place to continue that dialogue, I realize, is not in the hermitage, but at the junction of the hermitage and the world. Through the development of my own gifts as a teacher and writer I sense I can best work for both of us to bring to fruition some of those seeds that were planted between us during our human walk together. Further, since the material I bring into my life is also material I bring into his, positioning myself in this way provides him with a continuing stream of new impressions and a chance for him to exercise his own emerging gifts in these areas through his involvement in my creative process.

From my own perspective, this feels sometimes like a deliberate decision in favor of a certain imbalance in my spiritual development. If I were on my own, I would do it much the way he did, through a deeper immersion in solitude. But I have to trust that I am *not* on my own, and that whatever personal loss of depth I feel through an excessive trucking in those noisier energies of creativity is somehow being met and recalibrated in the deeper waters of his silence.

"For it is a young tree grown out of the old root which shall discover what the old tree hath been in its wonders," says Boehme.[2] This beautiful quote, in which the original German for "discover," *verklärte,* also means "transfigures" or "glorifies," very much describes the process at this stage of the journey. The sense of a common "root and sap between us" in the abler soul reassures me that the courage to bring forth my own gifts is also a bringing forth of his, and a growth of the tree for both of us. Not that I am completing what he left undone, but something far more organic: we are completing it together. As I am growing down here, spreading roots in the good soil of the here-below, Rafe is stretching his leaves and branches far skyward in the kingdom above. The two motions are the same.

THE BUSHWHACK OF BECOMING

But the truth of the matter may be much, much simpler...

In a small, out-of-the-way church in Campbell River, British Columbia, I came upon a quote pasted on a secretary's bulletin board entitled "Weaver's Prayer." "Dear Lord," it said, "My life looks like a mess of tangled knots and loose threads. But that's because I only see the underside."

It was a good reminder to me that the shape of our journey looks very different when seen from the topside, by God. Down here on the underside it looks like a candle and a wick. From above, it is pure flame. We struggle with the means and ends. God sees the quality of the aliveness.

This is talking tincture. From this viewpoint, the gifts themselves fall away to reveal the pure act of giving, and the journey toward completion is only the ever deepening act of becoming. And far more than those road maps of higher purpose, I find it is this dimension when I can genuinely open to it that gives the continued element of adventure and surprise to our walk together. It is where the growing edge really lies, I think—for both of us.

"You do not have to come all the way to me, because I am also coming to you." And I am struck sometimes by the obvious, simple truth of that. If it is love that calls forth essence, then the most helpful thing I can do for Rafe is to simply make space to let him love me. If in that night in the chapel he became at last a husband, then the best contribution I can make to him is to let him *be* a husband—in the literal Old English meaning of the term, "one who tends and nurtures."

"Take up your life and live it. And I will be there in the midst of it. There in your heart.

"Live your life as the gift it is...."

After nearly two years of hemming and hawing, I finally took the plunge and moved to British Columbia. When all had been pondered through, there was simply a gathering, incontrovertible·sense that this is what Rafe wanted. Why, I didn't know and still don't exactly. He had his own lifelong dream of getting there, but I think it was more a sense he caught, when I got back from that one teaching trip in spring 1995, "It was good for you!" A beautiful little hermitage came together, in a warm, gentle climate, surrounded by caring friends and a healthy balance of teaching and solitude. In accepting this gift, I sense I am also giving him the space to continue to nurture and love me as he was coming to do so well at the Stanley place. He sees what I need and gives from his heart. I respond with gratitude and relax my wary self-reliance. And so we tame each other.

As in the O. Henry story, it eventually becomes a chicken-and-egg kind of proposition. I want it because I think it helps him; he wants it because he thinks it helps me. After a while who gives what or why doesn't matter anymore; only the giving itself matters.

It is not without its comical moments and its real give-and-take. To leave Colorado was scary; there, every inch of the ground reverberated with the history of our human walk together. Alone, one day in late December, I was attempting to wrestle a dining room table out to the car to transport it down to the storage unit I'd rented. It was simply too heavy to move. I couldn't budge it; the person who had promised to show up to help hadn't. Tears of frustration rose in me: all the sense of aloneness and homelessness and fury. Finally I sat down and said, "Rafe, if you want me to go to British Columbia, you're going to have to help me yourself." Then I got up and moved the table into the car. It wasn't a great super-woman triumph, an adrenaline rush. Mostly it was suddenly seeing new angles—a way to slide it across the snow on a rug, inch-by-inch it into position, and then, just at the end, a little burst of strength to lift it up onto the tailgate.

And the shadow work continues, too—strange, but true: that sharing and exposing of the pain, the vulnerable moments. Rafe has held me as I cried in despair and frustration, but I have done the same for him, too. Of the many stories on this front, some too private to tell, the following one can serve the purpose.

I knew for a long time that there was something unresolved around that first hermitage experience of Rafe's in Waunita Hot Springs...something he'd wanted to process with me, but we never quite got to it in life. One morning about a year and a half after his death, I was seized with a strong sense of the time's being right to make a pilgrimage over there. I imagined it was a fool's errand. Waunita Hot Springs doesn't even exist on the new Colorado road maps. All I had to go on was an old photo of Rafe by a rock outcrop and a vague recollection he had told me it was twenty-seven miles to Gunnison.

As if by magic the way opened up. Eighteen miles east of Gunnison, a road sign pointed left to Waunita Hot Springs Ranch. And precisely nine miles down that road, I looked off a little to the northwest and there was the rock outcrop, looking on the surface like any of a hundred other outcrops, but from the inside literally beckoning in its intensity. I parked the car and headed toward it; fifty feet or so into the sagebrush, an overgrown and washed-out trail opened almost at my feet. Step-by-step I found my way into a well-hidden little gulch and onto the porch stoop of a tiny cabin. The door was unlocked. I walked in and found Rafe's navy pea coat still in the closet, and on the dresser a stack of unopened mail from twenty-four years before.

I'm not exactly sure what happened next. I sat down on a folding metal chair, and about a half hour dropped clean out of my life. When I came to again, it was late afternoon, the sun already dropping behind the ridge. From the tears in my eyes, I knew I had been crying. And I do remember some of it: Rafe saying, "Take hold," and somehow feeling something of the terrible loneliness he'd felt in this place, that "ache all the way to the end of the universe," and his bitter sense of failure at having finally run from it. Without knowing exactly what I'd shared, I knew I'd been let in on a slice of that terrible sadness he carried within him, and that in my willingness to carry it with him, something had lightened. It was a mysterious moment between us, and I walked out of that gulch with my heart aching and wide open. In times since then, walking blind in Louisiana and Mississippi, I have been led infallibly to the places of his deepest pain. And standing on the ruins, my heart cries out to him.

PURE FLAME

And so it *is* possible to keep the dance going between us, I discover—to continue on in the mutual becoming of love with a spirit of adventure and with raw, open hearts. The abler soul is not some abstract, esoteric concept. It is as real as two candles touching their flames together, melding the substances of their life through their common willingness to burn as one flame.

And slowly I come to discover that this one flame does have its own tincture, its own distinct quality of aliveness a little different from either Rafe or me alone.

Gentleness, joy, confidence, quietness: these would be some of the words I would put to these distinctly new flavors of ourself. The Sufis call it "finding your true name." And staying true to that true name—not the comings and goings themselves but a quality of being alive—is the one trustworthy way of staying on the path that love carves for us. Like sailing in the fog, you steer by scent and smell, knowing that they invariably point the way to the invisible harbor you seek.

For my part of the bargain, the requirement is to "stay in the way of the change," as Rafe liked to say toward the end, not bewailing last year's language, but reaching out to these new and more subtle signs of presence with faith and hope—and yes, obedience, the traditional wifely vow.[3] For it is only by my willingness to obey where I do not yet fully see that I can be led into the unknown territory that is love living itself into action. Beyond the grave there is only conscious love; only conscious faith, only conscious hope. It is the realm of eternal verities. But if I can allow myself to be led, I know I will be brought to my heart's true home, and even more, to the invincible certainty that this impossible wager is true: love *is* stronger than death and we *will* find our lives by laying them down.

CHAPTER 19

THE MYSTERY

OF CHRIST

I

XXX "BEAUTY," SAYS RILKE in his *Duino Elegies,* "is only the
XXX beginning of a terror we can just scarcely bear." And perhaps
what gives rise to the terror—and drives us to our stammering
attempts to describe and shape and assign purpose—is just this:
other than beauty itself, the Mystery has no shape; it can only be
borne by opening the heart more and more deeply. The heart is its
shape.

For all our great structuring and high sense of purpose, Rafe
and I both knew that the times most rich, most real between us,
were those when the veil of purpose got ripped away to reveal
something infinitely more unmanageable and immediate. When
we were knocked sideways, detached for a few moments from our
usual sense of self, as if the wind were knocked out of us. It happened to us most powerfully that last week of my stay at the Stanley place, when we finally had to abandon a scenario that would
have imposed a meaning on the situation but had nothing to do
with what we were actually feeling. At times like those—tentative,
thrilling, vanishing almost as quickly as they arose into heavier,

more familiar ways of being—there was a strange sense that we were being met...that something was drawing near to us, from a more profound order of reality, that somehow knew our hearts well.

In the second of his *Four Quartets,* T. S. Eliot wrote a set of lines that brought Rafe to complete attention:

> *Old men ought to be explorers.*
> *Here and there does not matter.*
> *We must be still and still moving*
> *Into another intensity*
> *for a further union, a deeper communion.*

What is that other intensity beyond the here and there that no longer matters? When I first met Rafe, and for a while afterward, he was still physically restless. Our early conversations revolved around his wanting me to help him move to a Maine island, a place of even greater remoteness, where he might give himself yet more intensely to the hermit's path he had chosen. Sometime in our two years together, with the help of T. S. Eliot and Helen Luke, he came to terms with that restlessness, recognizing that his "days of yondering" were over. Instead, and still with that spirit of adventure, he turned himself entirely toward the inner exploring, seeing what that other intensity might be. But you could never count on it to be there. Mostly it was boring and aging, things being harder, colder, tireder; sight dimming and muscles aching. And then occasionally, out of nowhere, something would descend, like an angel of that other intensity.

There was one evening, almost eventless in its own right, that somehow stands out in the constellation of my Rafe memories like a first-order star. It was late October, about six weeks before Rafe's death, with the first real snowfall of the season. Earlier that week he had brought his tractor and woodcart up the mud-slicked road for a major run-up on getting the winter wood in. We'd spent the afternoon together working in the woods, but I was dragging and a little sick, and although he was not in much better shape himself after an afternoon of chainsawing in the snow, he insisted on bringing me down the hill. He fired up the tractor, dusted the snow off; then, carefully laying an old poncho in the cart for me to sit on, he boosted me in, and we took off down the hill. Somewhere around the first bend, we both became aware of something extraordinary going on, as if this little voyage were suddenly trekking across the face of a far vaster deep.

Twelve hours later, the vividness still only barely receding, I tried to capture some of the feeling of it in my journal:

> Cold, snow…seriously winter again…and we are on the tractor, and Rafe is bringing me down the hill.…The little guy in his watch cap, alternately standing up and sitting down on the damp tractor seat. Me in the cart back behind, sitting on top of the snow on a green rain poncho, and the old tractor lurching happily along the well-loved road, soft but not deep in snow: a kind of bizarre flight into Egypt or journey to Bethlehem, it occurred to me.…And from out beneath the tattered, scuddy remnants of the storm, the night star—one… two! Rafe standing up, looking around, watchful, watchman—and Lord, how I never wanted that ride to end! For a timeless moment—like a slice from another order of reality— it glowed with the very fullness of God, the infinite vastness and tenderness to which all things here below obliquely point.

It was nothing new, just a quality of intensity, a deepening to everything. That beauty which is "only the beginning of a terror we could just scarcely bear" hovering near a heart not quite vast enough to contain it, a cosmos not quite real enough to encompass it…yearning, straining at the entrails…

When we reached the bottom of the hill, not much more was spoken between us. Rafe was as blown away as I. He helped me out of the cart and for just a moment we looked at each other—or perhaps more *through* each other, toward the quivering beauty, yet somehow the poignancy, of that other depth. "It's close," he said cryptically. Then, as the familiar world of monastery barnyard gradually returned, we brushed the Scout loose from its dusting of snow and went our own ways into the night.

I I

"This is my body, given for you…"

Somehow among my most precious memories of Rafe are the two of us standing in the communion circle at mass. Gathered around the altar, usually side by side, we would eat our bread and pass the cup one to the other. One time as he passed it to me, Rafe leaned close and spoke the words, "May we be to one another as Christ is to us."

Toward the end of his life, in the years I knew him, Rafe pondered almost continuously about Christ and was spontaneous and completely open in his devotion. It was not something he wore on his sleeve, but if you scratched the surface even the slightest bit, it was right there. One time a woman journalist on retreat at the monastery, either making conversation or seeking out a story, asked him, "So what does Christ mean to you?" Without missing a beat, he responded, "Everything."

Later I asked him more about that. Knowing how his first conversion experience was a profound realization of God, I wanted to know how and where Jesus had gotten so involved in it. "Oh," he said, smiling, "I guess you could just say it's a growing presence."

I knew a little bit about that myself, how this presence or person named Jesus Christ could gradually get a hold in your life at a level deeper and stronger than any logic, almost like a life growing within your own life, with a will of its own. I first encountered that presence at the age of twenty when I received my first communion totally by accident. No kidding! I had showed up at an Episcopal church one Sunday morning to hear an English boy choir perform, and the next thing I knew I was being ushered into a communion line—about as close to pure heathen as they come: unbaptized, unconfirmed, no preparation, no expectations. I was quietly walking back to my pew thinking, "Well, that's that," when suddenly I knew, "Well, that's *that!*" Quietly, not like some thunderous charismatic conversion, I simply knew that I had met my match; something utterly real, strangely compelling, strangely familiar, had entered my life that day. For the next few years it was internal warfare. In the face of this beauty I could just scarcely bear, I was truly terrified and fought against it with every outpost of my rational mind—my head jabbering protest while my feet walked me every day to noonday mass at the local parish church, where a wise priest asked no questions and simply gave me the sacrament. It took five years for my head to shut up.

I think of those years nowadays as I continue to take my place in the communion circle. It was the first time in my life I ever knew something from the invincible reality of my heart—knew it against all purposes and plans and scenarios, simply by the incontrovertible fact of its presence. It is exactly the same way I am now learning to know Rafe—beyond all logic and disputation, from that same place of inner knowing; that same undeniable presence. Many times in these past three years I have been particularly thankful for the Eucharist; it is the only comparable reality.

"This is my body, given for you." I look down at the piece of bread that has been placed in my hands. What is it? Bread? Body? Energy? All of the above? It is a piece of bread. And as I eat it, I sometimes feel it large and vast in me, now more than ever before, as a presence, an energy. "May we be to one another as Christ is to us." I feel Rafe there in the bread, in the body of Christ. The story of our life is somehow in that life, and the story of our life *is* that life.

"This is my body, given for you." And in that body given, I also recognize another body given. In wave upon wave the memories flood over me. The bodies wrestling that day in the yard, shell-shocked but not running. The bodies that held and touched and comforted and stood by each other in anger and despair. And those long, exhausting days of lugging wood, or clambering around in the chilly, cramped pump house down at the Stanley to get the water going again; and the laughter and joy, perched on our barstools, lifting our cups of cappuccino...those bodies. And the bodies that cared for each other in our times of illness; I bringing him water one day when he was out of his head with fever up at the cabin; he sitting up all night to keep the fire going and watch over me when I was struck down with the flu one bitter week in January. And then, as it came down to the end, as he saw his own strength fading and my life impaled on my unwillingness to leave him..."I laid down my life so my strength could be in you."

"This is my blood, shed for you." And by God, we did cost each other blood! The tears, the blowups, the giving and yielding, the wearing each other out as we wrestled against each other and against ourselves, learning how "to be to one another as Christ is to us." What do I know of the love of Christ that was not taught me by Rafe? The laying down, the pouring out, the pattern of His life, which became the pattern of ours. The whole life is somehow there: Rafe's life, my life, everyone's life, all pulsating through that small chalice, that tiny piece of bread. Perfectly contained, utterly vast.

"In Christ, body and power are the same thing," says Boehme,[1] and my mind boggles at the mystery lurking in that simple sentence. This bread, which Christ calls His "body," I experience here as power and energy, a connection to a profound and vivifying presence that fills my life. But just as well, what feels like energy from the vantage point of this life might actually *be* body from the vantage point of the next: the pure energy of love and compassion and creativity might be the "body" we wear in the next realm, and the body in which the cosmic Christ actually touches and meets us in our present state.

Rafe never said so—maybe because it was for me to find out myself—but I have come to wonder, are not the body of hope and the body of Christ somehow one and the same? This sap flowing through all things, both the vine and the branches, mysteriously and majestically present at the heart of all creation, weaving and binding together time and the timeless, form and tincture, heaven and earth?

In this world we carry it within us: that mysterious life growing within our own life. In the next, it carries us within it, and we ourselves become the mysterious life growing within *its* life. And so Bede Griffiths can truly say on his deathbed, "Receive the growing Christ." We die into His body and grow in it, and it grows with us. We consume it, meet in it, speak within it, put it on, become the new that is its pattern and our own, live it, act it, share it...all one...all here. We go to meet it, and it comes to meet us. We grow to our full stature in it because it itself is pure becoming, pure love.

I I I

"Have you ever heard the stars move?"

I looked at him sharply. In these last weeks of his life Rafe had grown completely fascinated by an account in a Laurens van der Post book of an old tribal chief who could hear the stars move. "Can you do that?" he asked me nearly once a week. I didn't know. Where does hearing begin? Sometimes, we both agreed, we could almost hear the alpenglow on the Red Ridge deepen to a cry, it cut so piercingly into the still, sharp night....Somewhere, at that root place from which all things emerge, before sound is heard, one hears by that which sound is made from.

At the end, Rafe listened...a lot...and peered more and more deeply into the heart of things. It was less and less struggle, more and more simply moving toward that space....We read *King Lear* together and laughed and danced our way through the beautiful speech in act 4:

> *Come, let's away to prison:*
> *We two alone will sing like birds in the cage:*
> *When thou dost ask me blessing, I'll kneel down,*
> *And ask of thee forgiveness: so we'll live,*
> *And pray, and sing, and tell old tales, and laugh*
> *At gilded butterflies...*
> *and take upon us the mystery of things, as if we were God's spies...*

And Rafe, growing suddenly thoughtful, peered intensely through the cabin window at the little wrens in the yard, the sunlight dancing through the aspen leaves...then said slowly and earnestly, "You know, there's only one Mystery, and that's the Mystery of Christ..." His words trailed off, back into the silence of whatever had captivated him. More and more in these last weeks as his own vision, his own high purpose and striving, got knocked away from him, he simply opened his eyes and saw. If that first seeing back on his brother's farm was more an intellectual realization, this new one was definitely *Mu!*—the Zen cry of enlightenment—a direct vision of the world as the transparent, transfigured body of Christ, dancing and shimmering in love. Each wren. Each leaf. Each of us. Each star.

"You have to experience duality for a long time until you see it's not there," said Thomas Merton shortly before his own death. "Don't consider dualistic prayer on a lower level. The lower is higher. There are no levels. Any moment you can break through to the underlying unity which is God's gift in Christ. In the end, Praise praises. Thanksgiving gives thanks. Jesus prays. Openness is all."[2]

In the very last long conversation we ever had, five days before his death, the subject came around to gratitude. We sat in the shop, drinking coffee, watching the swirling clouds clear to reveal the mountains shimmering in their new winter veils. Rafe paused for a moment to look out upon the whole scene, then continued, "I don't mean an 'Oh, lucky me!' kind of gratitude; it's something simpler...if you're quiet enough, as still as that mountain, you can hear in your heart their silent 'thank you.' The whole universe, if you listen in your heart—every blade of grass, each bird, each stone—it is all 'thank you.' We are born into 'thank you,' we die into 'thank you'...every step of the way is 'thank you.'"

Rafe may not have heard the stars move. But I believe he was hearing "the love that moves the stars and the sun."

IV

I remember that picture of him particularly vividly, sitting there in the shop on the old snowmobile carcass, his eyes flashing, almost and already one with that pulsing vibration of gratitude, that Mystery of Christ so mysteriously alive in the universe. More and more it was only music playing as almost before my eyes he slid into that other intensity. I watched him finally able to stare directly into the eyes of the Mystery, to see the tincture without the form, the quality of aliveness without the snakeskin; to dance so fully and vastly with that heart of the music, the sound of the stars he always wanted to hear, that he was, literally, exploded out of form. His human heart burst; he had outgrown it.

I try to keep that picture before me as I walk in this here and now. I try to remember what he saw there at the end or even squint to see it myself. Most of the time it is like squinting at one of those infuriating dot-matrix pictures; the dots remain dots and do not give way before my eyes to reveal the flower hidden in the pattern.

I do not often see the body of Christ hidden in the random dots of the universe. Mostly, this feels like in-between time, a kind of limbo where Rafe is there and I am here, the two of us separated by form. My usual sense of the world is that something is missing, something is not complete, and I find myself yearning for that final consummation, when my flesh, too, has been left behind and we are reunited in our resurrection body or bodies, whatever the subtle form may be. Till then I try to do my work and use my road maps to keep me on course. The high sense of purpose that was so much a part of Rafe's quest and that he imprinted so firmly on me has its shortcomings: it tends to split the world into higher and lower, into now and later. But it also keeps one moving forward—striving toward that fullness of being that can never be had by striving alone but will not come to pass apart from it. As the old Sufi proverb goes, "Not everyone catches a wild ass, but only a person who is actually running can hope to catch one."

Only occasionally, outrageously, do I hear the more remarkable

186 WALKING THE WALK

music: the quiet reassurance that nothing is missing; there is no place to get to because it is all already here—and indeed, how could the fullness of God be true fullness if it were not present in this very now? No, it is simply my eyes glued in the wrong direction. The Kingdom of Heaven is not higher but *aliver;* it is right here, just on the other side of that "terror we can just scarcely bear"; the only thing lacking to embrace it is the depth of our hearts. Like that sleigh tractor ride down the hill that night, it hovers just beside us, wanting only to pierce our veils, to carry us deeper into its own mysterious becoming....

"For you must realize," says Boehme, "that earth unfolds its properties and powers in union with Heaven aloft above us, and there is one Heart, one Being, one Will, one God, all in all."[3]

In those last days of Rafe's life, and then for us both together at the funeral wake, I believe we touched the hem of this one Heart. When all the scenarios, visions, cosmic purposes, and human posts fade to the stillness of hush, there is only love itself that sounds forth, the music that moves the stars and the sun. Finally you stop running—from or toward—and simply open your heart, and that other intensity swallows you in its embrace. And for the duration of that embrace, whether it lasts a microsecond or the rest of your life, you peer into that depth and see, with the utter certainty of your whole being, that it *is* the body of Christ—and that in it, all things *do* hold together.

And so as I walk my way in these "mostly" in-between times, I am mindful of both the promise and the task that lie embedded in those last words Rafe spoke to me:

"You'll see. Nothing is taken away."

A WEDDING SERMON

On July 5, 1997, high in a mountain meadow above Telluride, Colorado, my oldest daughter, Gwen Bourgeault, and Rod Rehnborg exchanged their marriage vows. I was honored when they asked me to be their wedding preacher and even more honored when the words I spoke, a distillation of all I'd come to know through the journey with Rafe, seemed to move many people gathered there that day.

Marriage was the part of the path that Rafe and I never got to walk out in human life, and in this there will always be a certain sadness. But the lessons we learned are there to be discovered by each new pair of lovers who dedicate themselves sincerely to the work of fashioning their partnership into a true spiritual union. In this spirit, my comments that day on the discipleship of love form the appropriate conclusion—and continuation—to this book.

It is a privilege to have two roles at this wedding: mother of the bride and wedding preacher.

It's easy to look at marriage as the culmination of love—the end point of the journey that begins with "falling in love." But as all of you who have ever been married know, and as you yourselves, Gwen and Rod, are beginning to discover—marriage is not the culmination of love, but only the beginning.

Love remains and deepens, but its form changes. Or, more accurately, it renews itself in a different way. Less and less does it draw its water from the old springs of romance, and you should not worry if over time these dimensions fade or are seen less frequently. More and more, love draws its replenishment from love itself: from the practice of conscious love, expressed in your mutual servant-hood to one another.

In making these vows of marriage, you become disciples on the path of love. It is a powerful spiritual path and if you live it and practice it well, it will transform your lives and through its power in your own lives will reach out to touch the world. What you really do today is to put your lives in the service of love itself: to let the material of your own selves—your hopes and fears, irritations and shadows, your intimate jostling up against each other—become the friction that polishes you both to pure diamonds.

But how to stay in touch with that power? At those times when stress mounts and romance seems far away, how do you practice that conscious love that will renew itself and renew your relationship? After all, if you are disciples, there must be a discipline...

Here is the one that works for me. And while it's particularly appropriate to married couples, it can be practiced by all of you, in all circumstances of your lives, if you wish to deepen your own practice of conscious love.

It's contained in one sentence—four little phrases—in that great hymn of love so often read at weddings, from 1 Corinthians 13:

Love bears all things, believes all things, hopes all things, endures all things.

If you understand and recognize what each of these four phrases means and entails, you will be able to practice conscious love in all circumstances of your life.

"Love bears all things…" But this does not mean a dreary sort of putting-up-with or victimization. There are two meanings of the word *bear*, and they both apply. The first means "to hold up, to sustain"—like a bearing wall, which carries the weight of the house. Love "holds up and sustains." You might say this is its masculine meaning. Its feminine meaning is this: *to bear* means "to give birth, to be fruitful." So love is that which in any situation is the most life-giving and fruitful.

"Love believes all things…" This is the most difficult of the four instructions to understand. I know a very devout Christian lady back in Maine whose husband was philandering and everyone on the island knew it, but she refused to see it because "love believes all things." But this is not what the words mean. "To believe all things" does not mean to be gullible, to refuse to face up to the truth. Rather, it means that in every possible circumstance of life, there is a higher and a lower way of perceiving and acting. There is a way of perceiving that leads to cynicism and divisiveness, a closing off of possibility; and there is a way that leads to higher faith and love, to a higher and more fruitful outcome. To "believe all things" means always to orient yourselves toward the highest possible outcome in any situation and strive for its actualization.

"Love hopes all things…" Generally we think of hope as related to outcome; it is the happy feeling that comes from achieving the desired outcome—as in "I hope I win the lottery." But in the practice of conscious love you begin to discover a different kind of hope, a hope that is related not to outcome but to a wellspring ...a source of strength which wells up from deep within you independent of all outcomes. It is the kind of hope that the prophet Habakkuk speaks of when he says, "Though the fig tree does not blossom and the vines bear no fruit, yet I will rejoice in the Lord." It is a hope that can never be taken away from you because it is love itself working in you, conferring the strength to stay present to that "highest possible outcome" that can be believed and aspired to.

Finally, "love endures all things..." But there is only one way to endure. Everything that is tough and brittle shatters; everything that is cynical rots. The only way to endure is to forgive, over and over; to give back that openness and possibility for new beginning which is the very essence of love itself. And in such a way love comes full circle and can fully "sustain and make fruitful," and the cycle begins again, at a deeper place. And conscious love deepens and becomes more and more rooted in your marriage.

It is not an easy path. But if you practice it faithfully and well, as disciples of love itself, the love which first brought you together will gradually knit you together in that one abler soul, which from all along, even before you were formed in the womb, God has been calling you to become: true man and wife.

NOTES

The Books We Used

One of the coincidences that most impressed Rafe and me was the way our libraries dovetailed. From about 1971 on, completely independently of each other, we managed to find our way to most of the same watering holes, and these common reference points were a tremendous help in our work together. They were also the first places I turned to in my quest to discover a road map for the second leg of our journey.

Since the principles of soulwork beyond the grave come largely from the esoteric tradition, many of the names mentioned throughout this book will be unfamiliar to readers in the mainstream Christian tradition, and it seems, if nothing else, polite to offer a few words of formal introduction:

G. I. GURDJIEFF AND P. D. OUSPENSKY: George Ivanovitch Gurdjieff, hailed by some as the greatest spiritual master of the twentieth century and dismissed by others as a charlatan, appeared in Russia on the eve of World War I offering a teaching he claimed to have gleaned in more than twenty years of searching (for the most part, in Central Asia) for living remnants of the ancient schools of spiritual wisdom he was convinced still guided the destiny of humankind. His teaching—generally referred to as the Fourth Way or "the Work"—is something of a Rorschach test: Sufis, Christians, and even Buddhists claim that its headwaters lie in their own traditions. A brilliant and convoluted mixture of ancient spiritual psychology, modern quasi-science, and mythical cosmology, it lays out a path toward conscious human evolution based on inner attention and the "harmonious development" of the three primary centers of human intelligence—intellectual, emotional, and moving.[1] For an excellent overview of the Gurdjieff Work and its influence, see Jacob Needleman's chapter, "G. I. Gurdjieff and His School," in *Modern Esoteric Spirituality*.[2]

Peter Demian Ouspensky, a noted philosopher in his own right, was Gurdjieff's most prominent disciple before their break in 1922, and his book, *In Search of the Miraculous* (New York: Harcourt Brace, 1949), is still the usual starting point for students of the Gurdjieff Work. When the Bolshevik Revolution forced the incipient Russian group into exile, Ouspensky eventually found his way to England while Gurdjieff settled in France; through these twin (but quite distinct) streams, the Work has continued to exert its subtle influence worldwide.

MAURICE NICOLL AND JOHN G. BENNETT: Nicoll and Bennett were students of Ouspensky and Gurdjieff, respectively, and among the most influential shapers of the second generation of the Gurdjieff Work. Nicoll's *The New Man* and massive, five-volume *Psychological Commentaries on the Teaching of Gurdjieff and Ouspensky* are deeply grounded in classic theology and contemporary psychology (he was also a student of Jung) and are the basic starting points for the journey into the Christian inner tradition. Rafe had a complete set of the *Commentaries* up at the cabin and read from them daily, along with his Bible; the two were his foundations for inner work.

Bennett, whose work is somewhat more individual and quirkier than Nicoll's, was fascinated by Gurdjieff's Near Eastern sources, and his *Mas-*

ters of Wisdom makes a powerful case for the Sufi influence in Gurdjieff's thought. His book *Sex*, which despite its bodacious title is really a study of the transformation of sexual energy, was another mainstay of Rafe's journey.

BORIS MOURAVIEFF: Mouravieff began as a loosely affiliated disciple of Gurdjieff's (a fellow Russian refugee of the Bolshevik Revolution, he was first introduced to Gurdjieff in 1920 by P. D. Ouspensky), but soon branched out on his own, claiming that Gurdjieff's teaching represented only a fragment of the original tradition and was hence inaccurate and often heretical. His three-volume *Gnosis* (first published in French in the early 1960s and republished in an English translation three decades later) purports to present the true version of the teachings, which he describes as "Esoteric Christianity," handed down directly from the Orthodox tradition of Mount Athos. Somewhat paradoxically, given the fiercely celibate climate of Mount Athos, his work is also the most complete exposition of courtly love as a spiritual path, and the way of transformation through mystical union with one's "polar being"—a path that he calls the "Fifth Way."

Rafe never read Mouravieff. He flipped briefly through the first volume of the set and said, "Life is too short."

JACOB BOEHME: Boehme was one of those who *came* to me. I had had a longtime hankering to dip into the works of this seventeenth-century German mystic and happened to mention it to Rafe, who brought me the monastery copy of Boehme's *The Way to Christ* at the beginning of Holy Week, 1995. As I read, I had the experience of nearly everyone who feels deeply attracted to this teaching: Boehme becomes a living presence—a wise teacher and a friend, who himself guides the way through the dense jungle of his prose to the breathtaking clarity that undergirds it. He has been the single most important mainstay to me as I have tried to put together the building blocks for an understanding of soulwork beyond the grave. His *The Forty Questions of the Soul* and *The Three Principles of the Divine Essence,* more than any other sources, have helped me develop the principles of "the vow," essence and majesty, and "putting on the body of Christ."

Meditations on the Tarot: This book was published anonymously in the late 1960s and has put off many Christian readers, who assume by its title that it must be New Age. In fact, it is one of the most profound mystical apologies for Christianity ever written, its author stating baldly in one place, "The more one advances on the way of free research for [spiritual] truth, the more one approaches the Church. Sooner or later one inevitably experiences that spiritual reality corresponds—with an astonishing exactitude—to what the Church teaches."[3] It is by now no secret that the author is Valentin Tomberg, a Russian hermeticist, who at the end of his life experienced a profound conversion to Catholicism and wrote this book as his magnum opus shortly before his death. It represents an extraordinary synthesis of his lifelong experience and deep spiritual understanding.

LADISLAUS BOROS (1927–1981): The sole voice of traditional Catholicism represented in these pages, Boros belongs to the school of contemporary European mystical theologians following in the wake of Teilhard de Chardin and Karl Rahner. His *The Mystery of Death* first appeared in German in 1962 as *Mysterium Mortis: Der Mensch in der Letzten Entscheidung;* it was translated into English and published by Herder and Herder in 1965. Later, while researching his biography for this book, I discovered that Boros, who had been a Jesuit priest, left the order in 1973, was laicized, and was married. It is as if the timeclock of that "total surrender that is love's" was already ticking in him when he wrote *The Mystery of Death,* gathering his relatively brief life into an extraordinary richness of experience and insight.

VLADIMIR SOLOVYOV (1853–1900): Solovyov was one of the most brilliant philosophers of the nineteenth century, a close friend of Dostoyevsky's, a Christian mystic, and the supreme metaphysican of erotic love.

In addition, Rafe and I were much sustained by literature, particularly the insights of the metaphysical poets. T. S. Eliot, John Donne, and Shakespeare were favorites—and also Helen Luke, psychologist, literary critic, and conscious woman, who died in 1995 at the age of ninety. Her exquisite little book *Old Age* framed Rafe's understanding of growing into age and was always the clarion that called us beyond ourselves in our work together, when we had painted ourselves into a corner by old conditioning and outgrown road maps. Her loving and wise insistence that the way emerges not out of what is highest in us but what is wholest held our feet to the fire in the difficult work of inner integration—and became the cornerstone of my understanding of soulwork beyond death.

Rafe never read Rilke—except for one quote about "living the questions," which he loved so much he copied it out by hand and put it between the pages of his Bible.[4] But Rafe could have written Rilke. If you want to taste the essence of the world of ideas he was operating out of during those years I knew him, pull down from the bookshelf a copy of the *Duino Elegies* or *Letters to a Young Poet.* It is like continuing a living conversation.

Further Reflections on the

Body of Christ

Rafe never said so—maybe because it was for me to find out myself—but I have come to wonder, are not the body of hope and the body of Christ somehow one and the same?

It is beyond the scope of this book to engage in an extended theological discussion of the mystical body of Christ. But perhaps a few brief elaborations are in order for those interested in pursuing the subject further.

First, with regard to the similarity between the body of hope and the body of Christ, let me begin by recalling the salient points in my description of the body of hope in chapter 10:

1. It is a living, palpable, and conscious energy that holds the visible and invisible worlds together and makes possible the most intimate communion between them.

2. It is not itself the individual resurrection body or essential core of a person, but it carries and sustains this core in its full individual particularity and enables it to grow.

3. It is universal, but our individual connection to it is made by crystallizing something within ourselves that can

directly receive it—our "second body," or "wedding garment."

I would submit that any or all of these points could be applied interchangeably to a description of the mystical body of Christ, or "the cosmic Christ," as it is often known nowadays. Functionally, what Rafe named for me as the body of hope dovetails precisely with the traditional theological categories of Christ as the mediator between heaven and earth... "in whom all things hold together."

Boehme also depicts salvation as "putting on the body of Christ" in numerous references. Readers are referred in particular to the twenty-first question in *The Forty Questions of the Soul*.

But how—as Christian theology claims—can the body of a single human person be seen as uniquely the cosmic ground of all creation? For a deeper insight into this question I return to Ladislaus Boros and *The Mystery of Death*.

As a fully human person, Boros argues, Christ would have followed the same journey to death as all human beings follow: a gradual narrowing of all of his human and outer energies in a convergence upon that moment of complete "ontological exposure" that is death, when the soul is cut loose from the entire physical and psychological matrix that has carried it to this point. This moment is also a moment of total presence: to the whole of oneself—"everything we have guessed at, sensed, and loved"[1]; the deepest reality of one's own heart—and also to the whole of the universe. The soul becomes in that moment "pancosmic," Boros argues:[2] it does not withdraw from the material world, but "thanks to the process of death the soul is given access to a more really essential proximity to matter."[3] He elaborates:

This earthly, empirical world of ours is nothing more than a corner of that essential cosmos from which the force for existence flows into our world just like so many individual drops present each but for a moment of time....Seen in this way death appears as a descent into the centre of our mother earth, to the root unity of the world—there where all the connexions end in one knot, where all spatio-temporal things join together, burgeoning on one root—down to the furthest and deepest of all that is visible. Perhaps one might express this reality with the single word "heart." In the metaphysical process of death the soul reaches "the heart of the universe," the "heart of the earth."[4]

There—and this is the core of Boros's hypothesis—"the soul takes hold of itself through the pancosmos"[5]; and in that place of utter and complete presence gives its final yes or no to God.

What then happened in the moment of Jesus' death? The very same thing. He became present to his own deepest self and present to the cosmos at its deepest "root unity." And when God fully human met God fully God and gave his resounding yes, it is as if a fissure that had run through the world since the first moment of creation—perhaps the fissure of createdness itself—was finally healed. Boros waxes lyrical on this point:

> At the moment of Christ's death the veil of the temple was rent in two from top to bottom, the veil, that is, that hung before the Holy of Holies. For Jewish mysticism and subsequently in the Christian interpretation of this mysterious happening, the veil of the temple represented the whole universe as it stands between God and man. This veil was torn in two at Christ's death to show us that, at the moment when Christ's act of redemption is consummated, the whole cosmos opens itself to the Godhead, bursts open for God like a flowerbud. In his triumphant descent into the innermost fast-

nesses of the world the Son of God tore open the whole world and made it transparent to God's light; nay, he made it a vehicle of sanctification.[6]

Meanwhile, when by the passage through his own human death Christ became pancosmic—totally present at the "root unity of the world"—the reality of the mystical body of Christ as the ground of all existence may be said to have begun.

"Perhaps this might help us to explain better," Boros concludes, "why our world is so deeply and mysteriously filled with the reality of Christ."[7]

Building on this foundation, it is but a short further stretch to see "the cosmos in its totality"[8] as the resurrection body of Christ, and our own salvation as a "growing together with the risen body of Christ":

> Free of all the "fleshly" constraints of time and place, Christ is able to reach the men of all times and places and make them members of his transfigured body—enable them to participate in his "pneumatic" [spirit-filled] corporeity.... The glorification realized in the resurrection, i.e., Christ's entry into the unimpeded, open clarity of being, is, therefore, an event in the scheme of salvation. It procures the condition for the possibility of our salvation because it enables us to grow together with the risen body of Christ, and this growing together with Christ is precisely what salvation is.[9]

Boros's profound insights coincide with my own most intimate experience of Rafe and myself being held together in the body of Christ—from its tightest focal point in the Eucharistic bread and wine to the widest pancosmic view of the whole universe as the living body of the one life of Christ. Bede Griffiths's final words, "Receive the growing Christ," are a profound expression of that mystical seeing: that nothing can ever fall out of Christ, and that in passing from one's own "fleshly constraints" into the "unimpeded, open clarity of being," it is the mystical body itself that grows larger and more vibrant.

But Rafe—or Bede—never "disappears" into Christ, any more than Jesus "disappears" into Christ. Each one remains a living cell, with its own unique and irreplaceable particularity. The Mystery of Christ is that it "holds all things together," not that it folds them all into one.

A Note on Reincarnation

In view of the admitted complexity of the abler-soul hypothesis, many readers will undoubtedly wonder why I do not handle the issue of continued growth beyond this physical body through the much simpler mechanism of reincarnation. If Rafe's growth is not completed in this life, could he not simply take another body and come back in another life?

My immediate response is that reincarnation is not a doctrine that Rafe himself believed in or processed his life in terms of. His understanding of the hereafter was shaped entirely within the parameters of traditional Christian teaching, and at one point he told me flat out that once his body had been cast away, he hoped never to take it up again. "It's *already* a hindrance to consciousness," he said. My preference, apart from compelling reasons to the contrary, is to remain within the basic frame of reference we both used in our human work together.

Within the greater Christian tradition itself, opinions diverge as to the compatibility of reincarnation with the traditional body of doctrine. Some say reincarnation was in fact once part of the teaching of the early Church and was later suppressed; others say it is antithetical to the Church's core understanding of resurrection. Within the inner tradition the split continues as well. Ouspensky, Nicoll, Mouravieff, and Tomberg all assume some form of reincarnation (or "recurrence," as Ouspensky calls it); Gurdjieff, Boehme, and Boros argue against it. The great traditionalist René Guénon (whose name has not previously appeared in these pages, but who has been in the backdrop of many of these discussions through his influence on Tomberg) was adamantly opposed to the doctrine of reincarnation and did his best to demolish it on metaphysical grounds.

My own conclusion is that reincarnation does not intrinsically belong to the Christian color palette, particularly in the line of inner development I have been following. Boehme was the deciding opinion for me. Here is why:

First, the soul does not come down and "take" a body, if the argument I have been developing throughout this book is correct. Essence is a unique and irreplaceable contribution of the body itself. Aspects such as one's sex, ancestral heritage, and physical type are not the "clothing" one wears in this life, but the matrix of essence and a nonnegotiable part of one's unique selfhood. What is commonly called "soul" arises out of the interaction between essence and Spirit—or between what I earlier referred to as the "sensible" and "intelligible" aspects of reality, form and particularity meeting pure divine idea. Soul is the unique and authentic outcome of this interaction. The metaphor of the candle and flame is again useful: the candle (essence), ignited (Spirit) and sustained by the invisible air (again Spirit), yields flame (soul), the goal toward which both are bent. But the tincture of the flame—its unique quality of aliveness, color, fragrance—derives from the candle. The tincture of the soul—the unique quality of its aliveness, burning in the timeless dimension of eternity—is what I believe Gurdjieff means by "Real I."[1]

Second, reincarnation fixes the "I" at the wrong level. The very notion of "my" continuance betrays a level of self-identity that arises from the ego, the self-reflexive consciousness that compulsively looks back on itself and views itself from the outside. Even in life we can go far beyond this superficial selfhood of the ego, realizing that our deepest "I am" is a mystery that can never be grasped by the self-reflexive mind, but only coincided with in the heart. The entire point of meditation is to take us beyond our mechanical identification with the egoic self and enable us to rest quietly in the presence of who we truly are.

Joscelyn Godwin, commenting on Guénon's teaching on this point in a recent article in *Gnosis* magazine, writes: "He knew that we all live most of our lives in the transitory and illusory realm of the ego. But this is no reason for the bad metaphysics of mistaking our temporary human personality for our true being, and the worse one of projecting that personality into the past and future as an 'I' that is reborn in other bodies."[2]

Third, reincarnation places undue importance on human life as the summum bonum of all existence and hence implicitly limits that divine thrust toward more subtle forms of manifestation, and the possibility of infinite dimensions of existence. Like the citizens in Edwin Abbott's imaginary *Flatland*, who can grasp only a two-dimensional reality, we are terrified at the vastness of divine creativity and cling to our static notion of recurrence in time rather than yielding to the possibility of dimensions of reality far beyond our ken. Guénon is entirely unsympathetic: "As soon as we die, we leave the human species behind forever; and if we do not like the idea, that is our problem."[3]

My difficulty with the doctrine of reincarnation, at least as it is usually presented in Western tradition, is that it is too static. It disregards that thrust into a different dimension that seems to be at the heart of divine creativity. Even in the image of the candle and flame, we see this thrust. It is what Boehme calls a counterstroke *(Gegenwurf):* the same thing in a different, more subtle dimension. The flame is the counterstroke of the candle. Real I is a counterstroke of essence. *The Duino Elegies* are a counterstroke of Rilke's brooding, yearning, unconsummatable life. Once this principle is grasped, that each level provides the raw materials for a transformation to the next level of subtlety,[4] and that divine creativity dances through this whole process and is this whole process, then the Christian concept of "the arrow of time" is seen in its mystical component, and the doctrine of reincarnation shows itself to belong intrinsically to a different paradigm—the nondualistic unity of the East.

This is true even for Rafe and me. While we may still be growing together, the place where this growth takes place is in the abler soul, which is already a counterstroke of our human lives—the next dimension of subtlety, made possible by our willingness to sacrifice our individual selves as raw material for the holocaust of becoming. In one sentence that is the gist of my whole argument.

All the religious traditions seem to allow for the possibility of one of their "enlightened beings" taking up a body again having once left it. But this is always under special circumstances for reasons of cosmic servanthood, not to continue developing its soul.

A Note on Sexuality

Erotic energy is also, obviously, sexual energy. And as J. G. Bennett and so many others have observed, sexual energy is the most potent energy of creativity and transformation available to human beings, and its very nature is to interchange modes of expression, sometimes like quicksilver. "In one creative thought a thousand nights of love come to life again and fill it with majesty and exaltation," says Rilke. "And those who come together in the nights and are entwined in rocking delight perform a solemn task and gather sweetness, depth, and strength for the song of some future poet."[1]

But the instructions for use of this volatile, powerful, all-embracing energy on the path of spiritual transformation are contradictory and incomplete. Schools exist which say that only through strict celibacy, strict conservation of the seed, can sexuality be put in the service of inner transformation. Opposite and equal schools say that the experience of sexual union forms an essence connection between the man and woman and is a prelude, if not in fact the sacrament, of union with God. These two opposite schools converge closely in Fifth Way teaching. Some, such as Mouravieff, insist that the path requires celibacy; others, such as Charles Upton, see sexual expression as part of the turf.[2]

Given the incomplete and contradictory state of the teachings available to us, it does not seem possible or even desirable to lay down ironclad rules. The parameters need to be worked out by each couple in terms of the givens of their own situation and their own highest striving. But as one moves toward this individual discernment, considerable guidance is available from within the path itself.

The Fifth Way path, remember, is one of complete self-giving, of radical self-abandonment in love. Love calls forth the reality of the beloved, and the act of loving calls forth one's own deepest reality, so that what emerges is a new creation in love, the fusion of hearts and wills in that one abler soul which is our true self and our imperishable destiny. The total outpouring of all that one is for the beloved—and not so much the beloved alone, but for the building up of that abler soul—is the Highest Good on this path, the yardstick by which the particular exigencies of each situation may be measured.

Sexual expression, if chosen, must be *clarified*. Its counterproductivity from the point of view of spiritual work is the tendency to trap the couple in the coarser instinctual energies, themselves impersonal and having a life of their own. "Lovers—were not the other present, always spoiling the view!—draw near to it [the Mystery] and wonder," says Rilke in his *Duino Elegies*. "…But no one gets beyond the other, and so the world returns once more." Sexual passion does, indeed, tend to "make the world return once more"—to keep us enchanted and hence firmly under the sway of mortal and transitory life. The only practical way to higher ground—to a clarified sexuality—is through a jointly embraced celibacy, at least for a time.

Celibacy, because it represents a redirection of tremendous transformative energies, already puts one in touch with higher and finer spiritual capabilities. It was through his experiments in this area, I believe, that Rafe learned how to extend and direct his heart at will within the body of hope. And since this is clearly the nature of the communion beyond the grave, it seems sensible to at least start to get the hang of it here.

But celibacy must be *purified* of avarice and self-protectiveness: that part which would hold itself back from complete self-giving in order to protect its own spiritual self-interests. In point of fact, that was the "narrow spot" Rafe and I always found the most challenging to negotiate: how to embrace a celibacy that was not at the same time a withholding of self, a flight into holiness; but was a complete and shared realization of "everything that could be had in a hug."

But it does exist. There is a celibacy that is a complete outpouring of sexual passion at a level so high and intense that every fiber of one's being is flooded with beatitude.

And there is also a sexuality that, clarified of its craving and attachment, is truly Eucharistic—"This is my body, given for you"—a drawing near to the other with all that one has and is; in conscious love; to give the innermost gift of oneself in the most intimate foretaste of divine union that can be known in human flesh.

Both exist. Either can be attained—or both can be attained—with pain, confusion, false starts, forgiveness, and grace—by partners who know that the only absolute law on this path is the law of absolute self-giving.

Chapter Notes

CHAPTER 2: THE ROAD NOT TAKEN

1. John S. Dunne, *The Reasons of the Heart* (New York: Macmillan, 1978), 141.

2. Among the spate of works, see Michael Baigent, Richard Leigh, and Henry Lincoln, *Holy Blood, Holy Grail* (New York: Dell Publishing Co., 1983); Margaret Starbird, *The Woman with the Alabaster Jar* (Santa Fe: Bear and Company, 1993); and the film *Jesus of Montreal*.

3. For a good introduction to this fascinating underground history, see Charles A. Coulombe, "The Secret Church of John," *Gnosis* magazine, 45 (fall 1997): 47–53.

CHAPTER 3: THE MYSTICAL COMPLETION OF SOULS

1. *Gnosis*—the term often applied to this body of inner teaching—is very different from "gnosticism," a first-century heresy property rejected by the early Church fathers.

2. J. G. Bennett, *Sex* (York Beach, Maine: Samuel Weiser, 1981), 54.

3. Boris Mouravieff, *Gnosis*, vol. 1 (Newbury, Mass.: Praxis Institute Press, 1989), 245.

4. For an excellent summary of this inner practice, see Jacob Needleman, *Lost Christianity* (New York: Doubleday, 1980), especially 166–68.

5. Maurice Nicoll, *The New Man* (New York: Penguin Books, 1981), 76–77.

6. Ibid., 78.

7. Jacob Boehme, *The Way to Christ* (Mahwah, N.J.: Paulist Press, 1978), 182.

8. Matthew 22: 2–14.

9. G. I. Gurdjieff, *Beelzebub's Tales to His Grandson* (New York: Triangle Press, 1992), 702.

10. Jacob Boehme, *The Three Principles of the Divine Essence* (Kila, Mont.: Kessinger Publishing Co., ISBN 1-56459-213-8), 480.

The citation in the text is my own translation of this passage, working from the original German as well as the standard English translation by Boehme's indefatigable seventeenth-century disciple John Sparrow. Sparrow's somewhat antiquated version reads as follows:

"It [the soul] may be comprehended as followeth: If it hath promised somewhat in the time of the body and hath not recalled it, then that word, and the earnest promise, comprehendeth it (which we ought to be silent in here); or otherwise there is nothing that comprehendeth it, but only its own Principle wherein it standeth, whether it be the kingdom of hell or of heaven."

For "if it hath promised somewhat," Sparrow offers the variant of "hath been enamoured" to convey the sense, implicit in the German *verloben,* that this promise is in essence a love bond.

11. Beatrice Bruteau, "Persons in Love," *The Roll* (quarterly newsletter of the Schola Contemplationis, 3425 Forest Lane, Pfafftown, N.C.), March 1996, 9–10.

12. Boehme, *Way to Christ,* 122.

13. "And nature with its wonders is a fiery sharpness, and taketh hold of

the eternal liberty [i.e., the eternal, unmanifest unity of God] and so maketh Majesty in the liberty through the wonders," Boehme writes in *The Forty Questions of the Soul* (Kila, Mont.: Kessinger Publishing Co., ISBN 1-56459-266-9), 144. I will discuss the significance of majesty, a crucial parameter in understanding soulwork beyond the grave, in chapter 14.

14. Matthew 25: 14–30.

CHAPTER 5: THE EAST LESSON

1. Hermann Hesse, "Stages," in *The Glass Bead Game* (New York: Holt, Rinehart, and Winston, 1969), 444.

CHAPTER 9: WRESTLING WITH AN ANGEL

1. Helen M. Luke, *Old Age* (New York: Parabola Books, 1987), 95.

CHAPTER 10: THE BODY OF HOPE

1. Valentin Tomberg, *Meditations on the Tarot* (Rockport, Mass.: Element Books, 1993), 471–72.

2. Ibid., 277–78.

3. Kabir Edmund Helminski, *Living Presence* (New York: Jeremy P. Tarcher, 1992), 118.

4. Fyodor Dostoyevsky, *The Brothers Karamazov* (New York: Viking Penguin, 1958), 427.

5. Bruno Barnhart, *The Good Wine* (Mahwah, N.J.: Paulist Press, 1994), 196.

6. Dostoyevsky, *Brothers Karamazov*, 427.

7. Helminski, *Living Presence*, 130.

CHAPTER 11: BUILDING SECOND BODY

1. *Unseen Warfare*, trans. E. Kadloubovsky and G. E. H. Palmer (Crestwood, N.Y.: St. Vladimir's Seminary Press, 1987), 244.

2. Nicoll, *New Man*, 143.

3. For an excellent overview of the Gurdjieff work, see Jacob Needleman, "G. I. Gurdjieff and His School," in *Modern Esoteric Spirituality*, ed. Antoine Faivre and Jacob Needleman (New York: Crossroad, 1992), 359–80. In brief, the three mainstays of the Work principles are (1) *inner attention:* the effort to be fully present to whatever one is doing, not lost in daydreams or emotional reactions; (2) *self-observation:* the effort to look objectively at "how one is" in any given moment, including habitual physical, emotional, and mental postures; (3) *self-remembering:* the effort to stay connected to a deeper and more holistic sense of self, rather than losing oneself in the kaleidoscope of personalities, contrary desires, and external distractions that comprise our usual sense of selfhood.

4. Jacob Boehme, *Confessions* (Kila, Mont.: Kessinger Publishing Co., ISBN 1-56459-214-6), 50.

5. Maurice Nicoll, *Psychological Commentaries on the Teaching of Gurdjieff and Ouspensky*, vol. 3 (Boulder, Colo., and London: Shambhala, 1984), 927.

6. Valentin Tomberg, *Anthroposophical Studies in the New Testament* (Spring Valley, N.Y.: Candeur Manuscripts, 1985), 135.

7. Ladislaus Boros, *The Mystery of Death* (New York: Seabury Press, 1973), 60.

8. Ibid., 61.

9. Ibid.

10. Ibid., 62.

11. Boehme, *Forty Questions of the Soul*, 189.

12. Hazrat Inayat Khan, *The Call of the Dervish* (New Lebanon, N.Y.: Omega Publications, 1981), 40.

CHAPTER 12: RAFE AFTER DEATH

1. John Cassian, *Conferences*, ed. Colm Luibheid (Mahwah, N.J.: Paulist Press, 1985), 49–50.

2. D. H. Lawrence, "Shadows," from *The Complete Poems of D. H. Lawrence*, vol. 2, ed. Vivian de Sala Pinto and Warren Roberts (New York: Viking, 1964), 226–27. Rafe undoubtedly copied the poem from Helen Luke's *Old Age*, 101–2.

3. Boros, *Mystery of Death*, 83.

4. Ibid., 164.

5. Ibid., 46.

6. Ibid., 55.

7. Boehme, *Way to Christ*, 182.

8. Boros, *Mystery of Death*, 83.

CHAPTER 13: DO THE DEAD GROW?

1. Boehme, *Forty Questions of the Soul*, 256.

2. Boros, *Mystery of Death*, 86–87.

3. "Love bears all things, believes all things, hopes all things, endures all things." (1 Cor. 13:7). For a fuller reflection on the meaning of this passage and how it can be used as a touchstone for spiritual practice, see "Epilogue: A Wedding Sermon."

4. Thomas Merton, "The Inner Experience" (unpublished manuscript, portions of which appeared sequentially in several issues of *Cistercian Studies*, 1983. Reprinted by permission of Merton Legacy Trust).

CHAPTER 14: ESSENCE AND MAJESTY

1. Boehme, *Forty Questions of the Soul*, 255.

2. Rainer Maria Rilke, *Letters to a Young Poet*, trans. Stephen Mitchell (Boston: Shambhala, 1993), 101.

3. Beatrice Bruteau, *God's Ecstasy* (New York: Crossroad, 1997), 31.

4. Boris Mouravieff, *Gnosis*, vol. 2, (Newbury, Mass.: Praxis Institute Press, 1992), 257.

CHAPTER 15: THE ABLER SOUL

1. The pertinent lines from Donne's poem, "The Ecstasy," are quoted at the beginning of chapter 1.

2. Vladimir Solovyov, *The Meaning of Love* (Hudson, N.Y.: Lindisfarne Press, 1985), 51.

3. Mouravieff, *Gnosis*, vol. 1, 131.

4. Rilke, *Letters to a Young Poet*, 81.

5. Mouravieff, *Gnosis*, vol. 1, 251.

6. *A Recapitulation of the Lord's Prayer* (anonymous, privately circulated publication), 88–89. The author was an English gentleman and student of P. D. Ouspensky's, who, along with a small group of Ouspensky's most committed disciples, was with Ouspensky at the time of his death. So moved by this event, the writer withdrew into solitude in India for more than a decade. This small volume represents the synthesis of his lifelong erudition and spiritual wisdom. By great fortune, a copy of it fell into my hands in June 1995, and of course I shared it with Rafe. It became his most important sourcebook in the three months preceding his death.

7. Charles Upton, "Love Embattled" (unpublished manuscript, generously lent to me by the author), 20.

8. The other major modern variant on this tradition is Jung's teaching on the animus and anima in which the "beloved" becomes a veiled image for individuation, the uniting of animus and anima (or male and female aspects) within one's own soul. Both Jung and Mouravieff would agree that: "Every man is born bearing within him the image of his polar being. As he grows, the image grows within him" (*Golden Book*, quoted in *Gnosis*, vol. 2, 254). But their interpretations are diametrically opposite. In the ancient teaching, the animus or anima is the inner image of the actual objective beloved—not, as is the increasingly popular teaching today, the reverse: that the person is merely a "projection" of one's inner archetype of wholeness.

9. For a full statement of this teaching, see chapter 3, "The Mystical Completion of Souls," page 34.

10. According to the ancient mythology, in an earlier, primordial sphere, the two beloveds were originally one soul; their "fall" into bodies represented a cleavage of their primordial oneness, and their needle-in-a-haystack reconnection on earth is not a meeting but a reunion.

CHAPTER 17: LOVE AND DEATH
1. Boros, *Mystery of Death*, 47.

CHAPTER 18: WORKING IN THE WONDERS
1. A phrase borrowed from the Fourth Way tradition to describe the full entrance into this mastery—or, in terms I have been using, the full maturation of one's majesty, up to the intended degree of luminosity. See Mouravieff, *Gnosis*, vol. 1, 54–62.

2. Boehme, *Forty Questions of the Soul*, 224.

3. I was quite pleased to have my instincts on this point confirmed by an observation in *Meditations on the Tarot:* "It is through obedience that the will is able to perceive" (p. 317; for bibliographical data on this work, see note 1, chapter 10). First one obeys, then one sees, and only finally does one come to understand. From the standpoint of soulwork beyond the grave, the traditional job descriptions of "husband" and "wife" contained in the marriage vows are not antiquated baggage, but precise descriptions of the path that must be followed.

CHAPTER 19: THE MYSTERY OF CHRIST
1. Boehme, *Three Principles of the Divine Essence*, 391.

2. Patrick Hart, ed., *Thomas Merton, Monk* (Garden City, N.Y.: Image Books, 1976), 90.

3. Jacob Boehme, *Confessions*, 41.

THE BOOKS WE USED

1. The intellectual and emotional centers correspond roughly with what in today's parlance would be called "the head" and "the heart." The moving center, perhaps best translated as "the wisdom of the body," includes both autonomic/instinctive functions and voluntary movement.

2. Needleman, "G. I. Gurdjieff and His School," in *Modern Esoteric Spirituality*, 359–80.

3. Tomberg, *Meditations on the Tarot*, 281.

4. "Be patient with all that is unresolved in your heart, and seek to love the questions themselves. Do not seek the answers that cannot be given to you because you would not be able to live them. But the point is: to live everything. Live the questions now" (Rilke, *Letters to a Young Poet*, fourth letter). I am not sure what edition Rafe was copying from; the punctuation is his own. For a comparison, see *Letters to a Young Poet*, trans. Stephen Mitchell, 49–50.

FURTHER REFLECTIONS ON THE BODY OF CHRIST

1. Boros, *Mystery of Death*, 164.
2. Ibid., 77.
3. Ibid.
4. Ibid., 78.
5. Ibid., 79.
6. Ibid., 150.
7. Ibid.
8. Ibid., 149.
9. Ibid., 157.

A NOTE ON REINCARNATION

1. This also clarifies to a considerable extent Gurdjieff's teaching, "Behind personality stands essence. Behind essence stands Real I. Behind Real I

stands God." It is also why Boehme can say, "The tincture is the true body of the soul" (Boehme, *Forty Questions of the Soul*, 123).

2. Joscelyn Godwin, "The Case Against Reincarnation," *Gnosis* magazine, 42 (winter 1997): 32.

3. Ibid. This is Godwin's paraphrase of Guénon.

4. I would prefer to say "to the next level of *artifice*," if the term can be understood not in the sense of "artificial," but as the product of a conscious creative process.

A NOTE ON SEXUALITY

1. Rilke, *Letters to a Young Poet*, 54.

2. Upton, "Love Embattled," 13–14.

Index

resurrection, of Jesus Christ, 100,
    101, 201–2
resurrection body, 90, 100–1, 185,
    201, *see also* body of Christ
rest, eternal, *see* afterlife
Ricoeur, Paul, 167
Rilke, Rainer Maria, 12–13, 49, 58,
    61, 136, 146, 176, 197, 205, 207,
    208, 217 (n. 4)
Rumi, 154

second body, 35, 38–41, 43, 90,
    104–14, 199
self-configuration, 90, 100–1, 110–
    13
self-surrender, 16, 123, 125, 131, 149,
    163, 165
"sensible universe," 91, 92, 204
sexual energy, 144, 149
    and creativity, 144, 207
    genital expression of, 36, 144, 208
    transformation of, 66–67, 68, 195,
        207, 208–9
shadow work, 38, 134, 136–39, 143,
    148–49, 150, 173, 189
Shakespeare, William, 24, 183, 197
Solovyov, Vladimir, 145, 146, 197
Song of Songs, 34
soul, 37–38, 204
soulmates, 143, 146, 151, *see also* abler
    soul
spiritual energy, 25, 65, 66, 67, 91,
    110, 144, 145
    in body of hope, 89, 92, 105
    in Eucharist, 181–82
spiritual practice (conscious work),
    76, 102, 104, 105–10, 114
    Rafe's, 107–10
spiritual warfare, 77, 156

subtle bodies, 36, 89, 110
    vital body, 113
Sufism, 106, 114, 175, 185, 194–95,
    see also Helminski, Kabir

Thomas, Dylan, 21, 81, 83
time, 43, 82, 98, 123, 127, 131, 135, 151,
    206, *see also* growth beyond
    death
tincture, 94–95, 97, 102, 113, 171, 175,
    182, 204
Tomberg, Valentin, 35, 91–92, 105,
    110, 196, 203, 204
transmission, spiritual, 145–46
true love, 16, 17, 32, 141–42, 147, 151
    and sacrifice, 147, 150, 165, 206,
        see also death

union of souls, 25, 35–38, 160, *see
    also* abler soul
Upton, Charles, 10, 149, 207

van der Post, Laurens, 183
vow, mystical/nuptial, 35, 41–43,
    142, 153, 160, 211 (n. 10)

wager, hermeneutical, 31, 44, 114,
    167, 175
wedding garment, 34, 39–40, 41, 43,
    83, 90, 104, 199
wholeness, 30, 35, 45, 83, 139, 141,
    142, 151, 157, 159–60, 169–70,
    197
"wonders," 35, 43–46, 90, 133, 134,
    167, 168
Work, the, 108, 194, *see also* Fourth
    Way

Permissions

About the Author

The Reverend Cynthia Bourgeault, Ph.D., is an Episcopal hermit priest presently living in British Columbia, where she divides her time between solitude and her role as resident teacher for the Contemplative Society. Over the past two decades she has visited, studied, and taught in Benedictine monasteries throughout the United States and Canada, while earning her "outside" living variously as a college professor, medievalist, editor, and parish priest. She is an oblate of New Camaldoli Hermitage in Big Sur, California, and a past Fellow of the Institute for Ecumenical and Cultural Research at St. John's Abbey in Collegeville, Minnesota. A regular contributor to *Gnosis* magazine, she is the author of many articles and audiotapes on the spiritual life (including *Singing the Psalms,* a 1997 release from Sounds True) and is an internationally known retreat leader.